LIFE WITHOUT COMPROMISE

John R. Bisagno

BROADMAN PRESS
Nashville, Tennessee

4215-03
ISBN: 0-8054-1503-3

Dewey Decimal Classification: 222.2
Subject heading: BIBLE. O.T. JOSHUA / / CHRISTIAN LIFE
Library of Congress Catalog Card Number: 81-71253
Printed in the United States of America

Contents

1
Prepared for the Battle

Joshua 1:1-18

The Book of Joshua in the Old Testament is the historical counterpart to Ephesians in the New. It pictures victory in the Christian life through the principle of faith and trust in the power of another. Jesus Christ, our heavenly Joshua, fights for us as did Joshua for the Hebrews nearly four centuries ago.

Comprised of twenty-four chapters it was written approximately 1,450 years before the birth of Christ and was probably authored by Joshua himself. It is significant as a picture of the principles which bring victory in the life of the twentieth-century Christian because it introduces the second section of the Bible, the books of history; and it is significant in the experience of the Hebrew people under Joshua's command.

One is immediately faced with the dilemma of Joshua, a book of battle, strife, and conflict as a picture of the Christian life. Its analogy is perhaps the most misunderstood of all the Old Testament books. Undoubtedly, the misunderstanding is created by the bad theology of some of our Christian hymns which say, "We're marching to Zion" and "I am bound for the Promised Land." These have suggested to us for decades that Canaan, Beulah Land, the land of Zion, the Promised Land, are none other than heaven itself. "On Jordan's stormy banks I stand, And cast a wishful eye To Canaan's fair and happy land, Where my possessions lie" indicates clearly that the hymn-writer was making Canaan the Land of Promise, a picture of the Christian heaven.

But there is no conflict or battle in heaven. The writer of the Hebrew letter stated in chapter 3, verse 11, that because of the rebellion in the wilderness the children of Israel were not allowed to "enter into his rest." How, then, can an obvious land of conflict be called a land of rest? Precisely this, that the Christian life was never intended to be a cessation of battle where conflict and spiritual warfare are the raw materials from which the fabric of success are woven for the Christian. Joshua's Canaan is indeed the battleground of the Christian's warfare, but it is a battleground in which the Christian stands at rest quietly, patiently, and victoriously as Jesus Christ, his heavenly Joshua, fights and wins the battles in his behalf.

The new believer is often surprised to find that his spiritual struggles not only continue, but actually increase in his new life in Christ. It is absolutely essential to understand that being a Christian was never intended to be a cessation of conflict. For without battles there are no heroes; without war, no victors; without struggle, no conquerors.

Paul exhorted young Timothy to be a good soldier of Christ and called Jesus the Captain of our salvation. The Christian life is a battle, but it is not our battle. It is to be regretted that following Christ is too often, to the disappointment of the new Christian, painted as a bed of roses. It is a conflict and yet it is peace—peace in the midst of conflict. We do go into the fiery furnace, but like the children of Israel, we find that we are accompanied by a fourth man in the fire like unto the Son of God himself.

As with the disciples, our Master thrusts us often into the stormy sea, for knowing Christ is not an absence of storms—it is peace in the midst of the storm, security in spite of the storm. And so, conflict and rest and peace and battle are harmonized in the life of the believer, both as illustrated by Joshua and as taught in Paul's New Testament writings.

And so, as we approach the Book of Joshua, let our mind-set be precisely this: That the principles for victorious Christian living as taught in the Book of Joshua are that through struggle (but it is not our struggle), through conflict (but it is not our conflict), it is his battle and he alone gives the victory.

The central spiritual truth in Joshua, then, is learning to appropriate all that is ours positionally in Christ, that it might become ours experientially. That which we know to be true may become experientially true as we see Joshua picturing our heavenly Joshua, none other than the Lord Jesus himself, our strength and our Defender.

"After the death of Moses . . . it came to pass" (1:1). Those are some of the most beautiful words in the world. Thank God that even in death, in impossible situations, in insurmountable problems, and unsolvable difficulties, it always comes to pass. God always has his way. Men come and go, but God is always there. The Lord spoke unto Joshua and said, "Moses my servant, is dead" (v. 2).

Herein is introduced one of the first great principles of the Christian life. Moses, who represents the law, can only go so far. Joshua, a picture of the Lord Jesus in grace, can alone lead us on to the Promised Land of victory. The law has served its purpose. The law was a schoolmaster to bring us to Christ. It has done its part; exit Moses, enter Joshua. Exit the law, enter grace.

The dead letter of the law can never save, but it points us to salvation; nor can it give victory, though it makes obvious the need. The promise of verse 2 is that the long anticipated day has come. Now, right now, stand up and go forward, victory's day is here, and it is victory in a land that I give to you and to the children of Israel. It is the fulfillment of a promise of over forty years standing, and all of it, verse 3 states, every square inch, belongs to you. God will keep his word.

In verse 4 the land is described and it is the covenant land promised to Abraham and his descendants in Genesis 12 and defined in Genesis 15. In verse 5 another important principle is introduced: the victory promised the people in verse 2 is a victory entrusted to another in verse 5. The people could stand only as Joshua stood. Their victory was victory in him. Our victory is Christ's victory. In him alone we stand, and the consistency of that victory will not fail. "As I was with Moses, so I will be with thee." Christian victory is not in struggle and effort; it is in rest and faith in him who fights for us.

The promise to Joshua was God's encouraging assurance that he would neither fail him nor forsake him and that Joshua could, therefore, be strong and of good courage, for God would do His work. The Christian today longs to hear no word more than that—that everything is all right, God is in control; therefore, be of good cheer and of strong courage. But this brings us to the qualifications for God's presence and victory in our behalf.

Verses 7 and 8 give the first qualification: Obedience. Four ingredients to obedience are recorded, and they all relate to unswerving response to the will and Word of God. First, observe all the law. Second, turn not to the right or the left. No exception and no variance. Third, the Word of God must never depart out of your mouth. This does not mean that Joshua or today's Christian must be spouting Scripture constantly, but that all one says as an expression of what is in one's heart must constantly be savored with the grace of God's Word. Fourth, you shall meditate therein day and night. The last thing before sleep, the first thing in the morning, and the main thing all through the day is to read, memorize, examine, quote, practice, and stand on the changeless Word of God. At the end of verse 8 God said, "Then thou shalt have good success." Here, then, is the first of the two basic principles for Christian success, obedience to the Word of God.

The second is in verse 9. Again, the prescription has four parts: be strong—be courageous—do not fear—don't be depressed. How can a person have such a positive mind-set as this? Every psychiatrist on earth would like to ensure their patients of these four mental qualities. But they are directly related to that which has immediately gone before; namely, obedience to the Word. Absolutely believe, perfectly commit your mind to the fact that everything is all right, everything is beautiful, no sickness, no discouragement, no fear, no depression. What is he saying? "Have faith in God." He has it all under control. Don't worry about anything. Everything is all right.

Here, then, is the second principle which lies in the basis of Christian victory: have faith in God. Obedience and faith are inseparable. How can I have faith in God? By obeying his Word and learning experientially that God may be trusted. And how can I demonstrate my faith? By obedience to his law. The main way I can show my absolute faith in someone is to act out my faith in obeying their wishes. Faith and obedience, then, stand together. I must trust someone to obey them blindly, and I must obey them to prove my trust.

Upon hearing the command of God, Joshua immediately commands the people in return (v. 10). God has promised to be with him as the leader of the people; Joshua believes God and acts instantly. Authority has been granted him and he will exercise authority. Herein is another extremely important ingredient in the Christian life: to have authority, we must be under authority.

Jesus Christ volunteered to go to the home of the centurion to heal his daughter. But the centurion said to Jesus, "You don't need to go. Just speak the word at a distance and she will be healed." In essence he was saying, "You see, I, too, am a man under authority. I understand the chain of command. I understand the concept. I give men orders and they obey because I take my orders from the emperor who gives me authority. I know that you, too, can order this fever to leave my child because you are under the authority of your faith." Jesus marveled and said, "I have not seen such great faith even among the Jews of Israel. Go thy way—thy daughter liveth." And she was healed from that very moment.

If you have no authority over your own life and the lives of your family and children, it may well be because you are out from under the authority of Christ, who gives you authority.

Having received the command, Joshua now commands the leaders to command the people to prepare victuals, getting ready for the battle (v. 11). Victuals are food, and the believer's spiritual food is the Word of God. Advance preparation is always required for spiritual conflict. You cannot have victory any day that you do not partake of the Word early in the morning. The preparation comes in advance. The specific time of victory is stated as just three days hence. Three days pictures the resurrection of Christ from the dead, and it is in union with the resurrected Christ, the Living Word, who takes the victuals that we have appropriated of the written Word, and wins the victory in our behalf.

While it is true that victory is possible in the midst of

conflict—only by grace, entrusted to another and qualified by obedience and faith—it is also true that the experiencing of that victory is possible only to those who commit themselves to follow our Lord.

In verses 12-15 Joshua reminded them that there is a choice to be made by those who will enter the Promised Land. Months before, the tribe of Reuben, the tribe of Gad, and the half tribe of Manasseh had opted not to enter the Promised Land, but to stay on the other side of Jordan. Though for a period of time they must aid their brothers in the conflict, God would honor his promise to allow those two and one-half tribes to return to the other side of Jordan. You may know Christ as your Savior and actually be born of his Spirit, but whether you go on to full maturity in Christ is yours for the choosing. What a pity that so many choose to never enter into the full blessings of victory that are theirs in Christ.

Some will indeed be saved so "as by fire." Verses 16-18 record the response of the people to Joshua's assertion of the authority granted him by God. The response was threefold. First was instant obedience. "All that thou commandest us we will do" (v. 16). Secondly, support. "Whosoever . . . rebel against thy commandment, . . . shall be put to death" (v. 18*a*). Third, encouragement. "Be strong and of a good courage" (v. 18*b*).

It is often said that great pastors do not build great churches, but great churches build great pastors. What undershepherd would not be pleased to have such a marvelous congregation as this to follow, to support, and to encourage him? A careful look, however, reveals one important qualification to their willing response (v. 17*b*), "Only the Lord thy God be with thee, as he was with Moses." "Yes, Joshua, we will follow you as we followed Moses, but we had better see God's power in your life as we saw in Moses'. To be under your authority you will have to demonstrate that you are under God's authority.''

I have often wondered if pastors who complain of having rebellious, troublemaking congregations are not simply proving, to their own shame, that there is no touch of heavenly authority and divine fruit in their own impotent and barren ministries.

2
The Conversion of a Prostitute

Joshua 2:1-24

Joshua had learned his lesson well. When Moses first sent the spies to check out the Land of Promise, only two returned with faith in God and gave positive report. The majority is not always right. At the first recourses a serious mistake was made. God never intended that the twelve spies attempt to determine *whether* the land could be taken. That was a foregone conclusion, for God had promised. They were sent to determine *how* to take the land, but only two returned to say that it could be done. Joshua was one of those two.

Undoubtedly, he selected two of his strongest men, and this time not twelve but two went to Canaan. Two witnesses agreeing together became the Hebrew tradition for establishing truth. "In the mouth of two or three witnesses, shall every word be established" (1 Cor. 13:1). Our Lord himself sent out his seventy to witness by two and two.

In the very first verse of chapter 2 we are immediately faced with the problem, "What were two nice Jewish boys doing in a Gentile house of prostitution?" For what, in fact, was Rahab's house? I submit that there are four possibilities: (1) They went there by accident. I rather doubt this, for they were obviously the best-trained of all the spies that Joshua had. (2) They went there to fool around. This theory, too, must be discarded, for Joshua selected his two best men; surely if anyone were to be trusted it was these two. Joshua, in his first responsibility, would never have made the mistake of selecting the wrong men. He had long since learned the lesson of forty years' suffering by just such a group of mistaken men. (3) They might have gone there because it was a good listening post . . . Rahab's house was on the wall, affording a lofty, prestigious location. If it was a house of prostitution in such a place, only the rich and the famous, the leaders of the community, could have afforded to go, and it would have been a marvelous listening place to hear about life in Jericho. (4) It's my belief they went there by divine appointment. They went there led of the Spirit of God because this was the only godly woman in Canaan who would cooperate with them, for she was, in fact, not the harlot Rahab, but the *ex-harlot* Rahab.

Her profession of faith is eternally preserved for us in verse 11. "The Lord your God, he is God in heaven above, and in earth beneath." In verses 9 and 10 the author has recorded for us the beautiful picture of how her conversion had come about. "We have heard how the Lord dried up the water of the Red sea for you" (v. 10). She had heard the testimony of Jehovah's great work and had believed and committed herself to him. There was no question in Rahab's mind that this Jehovah God was the only God of heaven and earth. We believe for many other reasons that she was a worshiper of Jehovah—possibly the only one in Jericho.

For one thing, why did the king, in verse 2, send men to her house to look for the spies? His intricate network of spies had brought him an accurate account of their presence in her home.

He knew that they were there, that they came under cover of night, that they were of the children of Israel, and that they came to spy. Where else would they go? It was natural for him to look there because he, too, knew that she was kindly disposed to the Hebrews. By her own testimony, her heart melted within her when she heard of the Hebrews' exploits. If she was not converted by the time the spies arrived, she must have been by the time they left.

Since Rahab had been a maiden catering to the rich and famous, her conversion had obviously rocked Jericho and had a great impact on a pagan community. There was no doubt in the king's mind that if two spies from the people of Jehovah had come to Jericho they would go straight to Rahab's home. We must believe further that she was the ex-harlot Rahab, worshiper of Jehovah, because she risked her life for these men. Willing to die for their safety she expressed her great faith. God, in return, would provide for her safety when the invasion began and her faith made the risk worthwhile.

Another extremely interesting insight into the case of her conversion is recorded in verse 6 where she hid the men on her roof under stalks of flax which she had laid in order. It would have been a long and laborious effort for her to have gathered flax, carried it to her roof, and arranged it in orderly stacks sufficient to hide two grown men. Flax is used in weaving material. She was obviously in the dressmaking business, perhaps for a long time, changing from her old life of prostitution to a new and honorable life as a dressmaker.

Further support is given in verses 15-18. She lived on top of a wall twenty to thirty feet high and let two grown men down all the way to the ground by a scarlet thread (v. 18). A piece of scarlet thread or rope long enough to reach the ground had been woven from a type of material from which five to six inches would have been cut as a dye piece in dyeing a batch of flax in a vat of hot water. And she had enough so that it was strong enough to drop two grown men thirty feet. Rahab was in the dressmaking business in a big way.

Rahab had been a believer for a long, long time. To this day we continue to observe the practice of calling people by their final title, the President of a country is referred to as Mr. President for life, even though he is out of office; the same is true of a captain, a general, or a senator or governor. But we do Rahab a disservice in continuing to refer to her as the harlot Rahab. She is the ex-harlot Rahab, and we would do well to extend to her the courtesy of referring to her simply as Rahab.

One is impressed in reading the roll call of the faithful in Hebrews 11 to find Rahab's name, but she was, indeed, a woman of great faith. The tenth verse bears her own testimony that she had only heard what the Lord had done and she had believed. It was and is by the hearing of faith and our response that we are justified before God and that we grow on from justification to sanctification.

Rahab, this beautiful woman of faith, evidences the touch of God on her life by her tender compassion for others. Her first temptation might have been to leave with the spies. That would have been a selfish act, and quite unlike a great woman of God. Immediately she thinks of her family. That they might know the salvation of the Lord as does she is of primary concern to her. "Shew kindness unto my father's house, and give me a true token: and that ye will save alive my father, and my mother, and my brethren and my sisters, and all that they have, and deliver our lives from death" (vv. 12-13), is her plea.

Only a token, just a gesture was all she required. She whose great faith had brought her to Jehovah knew that once Jehovah's servants had given her the slightest token of their guarantee, they would be eternally bound to their word, and her family's safety was ensured. Oh, the goodness of Rahab's faith and the changeless truth that by faith we are justified, and by faith we live.

The covenant was confirmed by the promise to drop a scarlet thread from the window, which thread, when seen by the onrushing army, would secure her salvation and her family's. It was the scarlet blood of an innocent lamb that secured safety on the night of the Passover. It was Rahab's scarlet thread that provided for their security, and it is the scarlet blood of Christ alone which secures our safety against the wrath of God. There is power in the blood.

Let us return for a moment to verses 15-18 where the writer clearly states that her home was on the town wall, and there she dwelt. In all likelihood, this unusual position of prominence and prestige had been ensured to her as a descendant of some earlier potentate in Jericho. It was extremely unlikely, indeed, for a private dwelling to be on the city wall, but the writer has made it clear that we understand that it was there. And it is positively affirmed for an important reason. Remembering that her house was on the wall, let me remind you that in chapter 6, verse 20, at the destruction of Jericho, all the walls fell down flat. Verse 22 of the same chapter, however, records that Joshua, after the destruction of the walls, sent the two spies into the harlot's house to bring her out with her family as they had promised.

If all the walls fell flat and her house were on the wall, how could her house still be standing for the spies to enter into as stated in 6:22? Obviously, most all the walls fell down, but God miraculously preserved a tiny portion of the walls of Jericho where Rahab's house stood.

In 1972 when visiting Israel we were directed to a remaining portion of the wall of Jericho. It is a thick piece of wall still several feet high unearthed by archaeologists. For many years I was disturbed, for I understood that all of the wall fell down.

Then it began to be revealed to me that this was quite obviously the remaining portion of the wall which miraculously stood where Rahab's house was built. Archaeology has confirmed what Scripture has stated: that even amid the judgment of God, his people may dwell safely under the scarlet thread of his blood and the shelter of his faithful promise. Faith in his blood and in his Word, and obedience to his command ensures our victory still.

3
Crossing Over with God

Joshua 3:1-17

"And Joshua arose early in the morning" (3:1*a*). This was the long-awaited day. Crossing the Jordan was the last barrier to the Promised Land. Years before God had promised Abraham to give his descendants this very possession, and at last it would be theirs. The Abrahamic covenant had provided for the Messiah—that the Hebrews would be a blessing to the world; for divine protection—"Curse them that curse you"; for physical and spiritual blessing—"Bless them that bless you"; for worldwide fame—"You shall be a great people"; and for a land—described in Genesis as Israel today.

One may speculate on Joshua's early rising. Perhaps it was to pray or to plan. But most likely, this long-awaited day had filled him with such great anticipation that he had hardly slept through the night and was awake very early to greet the day. First (v. 1), they would remove from Shittim to Jordan. Encamped in Shittim on the Moabite plains they could look across Jordan and, in all probability, see Jericho. Jordan was the next great obstacle, and there was distance between where they were and where it was, between Shittim and Jordan. They had no idea how they were going to cross that river. One thing they did know—it could not be crossed from Shittim. They must at least leave where they were. They had to get up against Jordan. They must do at least that much.

God will never do what he can do before we do as much as we can. His opportunity awaits at the end of our extremity. Never will he act until we have been faithful to do what we can. The command at the river was precise and simple: when you see the ark of the covenant carried by the priests, go after it. The ark was symbolic of the principles of God.

In the ark were three things: the tablets of stone bearing the Ten Commandments, manna from the wilderness, and Aaron's rod which had budded. The law spoke of obedience; the manna, of provision; the bud, of power. To know the provision of God demonstrated by the power of God, there must be obedience to God. Follow God, follow the ark, obey him, and he will provide your need by his power.

The command was to follow exclusively after the ark. The direction of God was of supreme importance. When the ark moves, you move. If it turns to the right, you turn to the right. Move when God moves, and stop when he stops. Go neither ahead nor fall behind. As God had been with Moses in the pillar of fire by night and a cloud by day, so he would be with Joshua and the people again.

The command in verse 4 was to stay about two thousand cubits from the ark. Approximately one-half mile distance must be kept between the people and God. Close enough to follow, but not close enough to breed familiarity and give birth to contempt. Jesus showed us this when he taught us to think of God as a loving heavenly Father, but added quickly that his name is to be hallowed.

Distance must be maintained to keep the right perspective of

God, but also to have a full view of the miracle God would perform. This generation had heard only about the miracle of the Red Sea, but an entire disobedient, unbelieving generation that had seen it was now gone. The Hebrews desperately needed their own validation of God and his Word. And so God would act again. The miracles at the Jordan River would be the most important agent in their lives. As the first generation to inhabit the land, it was essential that the perpetuation of their religion, which would give birth to the gospel for the whole world, be strongly rooted in the foundation of their own faith in God.

They must, of course, be prepared, and the directive was, "Sanctify yourselves: for to-morrow the Lord will do wonders among you" (v. 5). The word *sanctify* simply means to set apart for a holy purpose. I fear that there are many of us who long to see God's holy purpose for our lives—the miraculous demonstration of himself in our world—but who never set ourselves apart unto him to ensure that purpose. There is a high price to be paid for God's blessing.

It is interesting to note at this juncture that Joshua himself did not specifically know that God was going to repeat the miracle of the divided waters. God's promise in verse 7 is the repeated guarantee that he would be with Joshua precisely as he was with Moses. Undoubtedly, the heart of Joshua beat fast with anticipation as he began to understand that God was going to repeat the precise same miracle in the waters that he had done before.

Faith is turned to sight when that which he suspects is now confirmed. "Ye shall stand still in Jordan" (v. 8). God's promise to Joshua was security on dry ground in a divided Jordan. Joshua's guarantee to the priests was precisely the same. Somehow we are gripped with a sense of spiritual ecstasy at the words "stand still." It is as though the believer can laugh at Satan. In the midst of the greatest obstacles of life,

God will hold back the waters. We can walk through the valley of the shadow of death unhurriedly and unafraid because God's power enables us to stand still with serenity, composure, and victory in each impossible situation.

When I was a young man, I used to say, "I believe all of the Word of God," and I believe I did. I believed it because my heart wanted to believe, because it was right to believe, and because I had heard the testimony of others who had trusted God's Word and found him faithful. But now, years later, I can say that I believe his Word on the basis of my own experience as well.

To date, the miraculous power of God was only hearsay to that generation, but now they would see it. Now they would hear the word of the living God and experience its validating power. And Joshua said, "Hereby ye shall know that the living God is among you. . . . Behold, the ark of the covenant of the Lord of all the earth passeth over before you into Jordan" (vv. 10-11). Today you will see, today you will know. You have believed, you have followed, you have obeyed, and today your faith becomes sight.

It is the oft-repeated posture of Scripture to present the Lord to his people in precisely the manner in which they need him, and at the right time. The immediate problem of the people was not a financial, psychological, or philosophical one. It was a problem of nature. Dirt, water, rocks, sand, the physical world around them and immediately before them was their problem—the mighty Jordan River rushing at millions of cubic feet per minute.

It is precisely to this issue that Joshua speaks. "The ark"— his presence; "of the covenant"—his promise; "of the Lord"—his power; "of all the earth"—his control; "passeth over before you" (v. 11). Your destiny in the river is in the hands of the eternal, faithful, promise-keeping God who is

Lord over all the physical elements of this whole wide world. What you need him to be, remember that he is unto you this day.

I consider verse 12 a parenthesis and it probably belongs in chapter 4. I will place it there later.

The miracle at Jordan in many ways was mightier than the miracle at the Red Sea. The generation that came out of Egypt had seen the miracle of the ten plagues before that of the Red Sea. These people had seen nothing. At the Red Sea the waters divided before they walked across, but God was expecting more of this faithful generation whom he would trust to bear the gospel to all generations. He would part the water for them only after they exercised their faith by placing the soles of their feet therein (v. 13).

Those to whom much is given also have much required of them and God honors the faith of those who trust him. Let the record further show that God did not need the priests to touch their feet to part the waters—*he could have done it without them, but they had to learn that they could not do it without him.*

Verse 15 states that the crossing occurred at harvesttime when the river was flooding. Many liberal theologians have followed their accustomed silly, humanistic logic in suggesting that the Red Sea was crossed at a narrow, marshy point when the water was low. Of course, they never proceeded to tell us how Pharaoh's army was drowned in a marsh! But here the Scripture is specific in declaring that they crossed where the water was flooding and overflowing its banks.

The question naturally arises, Why did God wait until the waters were the deepest, rather than allowing them to cross in the springtime when the river was at its lowest level? Our Lord often allows the difficulties of our lives to compound themselves to the point that they have no obvious human resolution.

In just such a condition, God's power may be displayed the greatest, and our faith in him strengthened the most.

Weary pilgrim, do not dismay when our Lord is slow to answer. He is waiting for the maximum opportunity to bless you, to rescue you, and strengthen you with a glorious display of his grace that will make you love him and trust him more.

Verse 16 makes an interesting addition to the record of the miracle. The Jordan River dried up before the children of Israel as far as from the city of Adam to the salt sea. At the point of the crossing between the plains of Moab and Gilgal it is approximately forty miles to the north to the city of Adam and twenty miles to the south to the Dead Sea. The river dried up for sixty miles. As the Israelites were organized well enough to hear all the commands of Joshua and proceed in an orderly fashion, a one-mile width, at the most, would have been quite sufficient for the crossing. The obvious question, then: Why the other fifty-nine miles? We shall subsequently see that it was for the benefit of the pagan people and their spies, who were carefully monitoring every detail of the miracle, that this tremendous extravagance of power was allowed.

God's purpose with the heathen in Canaan was then, as now, that the ungodly should come to repentance. The miracle was for their benefit. Unfortunately, just as all in Jericho did not respond like Rahab when they heard of the Red Sea, neither did the unbelievers who witnessed the miracle at Jordan respond.

Chapter 3 closes with a flourish of praise to Jehovah, "And the priests that bare the ark of the covenant of the Lord stood firm on dry ground in the midst of Jordan" (v. 17). The Israelites passed over safely because the priests stood in the middle and God held back the waters as he had promised.

Oh, what a glorious sight—our Lord Jesus, our heavenly Joshua, our eternal High Priest, stands in the middle of our impossible rivers, hands extended, holding back Satan's on-rushing waters from all who trust and obey. Victory is in the midst of the battle. Peace and security are on the dry ground of impossible rivers because Jesus stands there and we stand with him.

4
God Keeps His Promises

Joshua 4:1 to 5:15

We are going to deal with chapters 4 and 5 as a unit and rearrange the six central events of these two chapters. These six events all happened at a place called Gilgal. Verse 19 of chapter 4 names the place, and the last verse of chapter 15 defines it as a holy place. Gilgal became tremendously important in the lives of the Hebrew people. It was the first piece of physical possession that they could actually touch and hold and say, "This is ours. This our God has given us as he promised."

As you recall, a part of the covenant was the land of Canaan. Upon emerging from the river Jordan their feet first landed on the shores of Gilgal. There they would regroup before beginning the conquest of the land of Canaan. It was, indeed, holy land, and it was to Gilgal that Joshua would repeatedly return throughout his ministry for regrouping, redirection, and rededication. Those first things in our Christian lives are extremely important to us and to those basics where first God became real, we do well to often return.

The word *Gilgal* means "thy reproach is taken away." It is

God's way of saying, "Open under new management." Things were different now. It was a new day for them. The scorn of 430 years of slavery was behind them. The tragedy of forty wasted years in the wilderness was no more. Things were different now. They were here in the Land of Promise, and it was a significant day in their lives. Gilgal, on the opposite side of Jordan, was probably about four or five miles from ancient Jericho. There the people could perhaps see the city.

Jericho was their first huge obstacle. To conquer Jericho would build strong faith and be a tremendously important initial step in the victory that God would provide. However, the time to conquer Jericho was not yet. First there must be a time of remembering the past. Monuments must be raised; lessons learned and thought through; commitment assured; and instructions clarified. Just so, God does not rush the new convert into the hard battles of the Christian life. New wine must not be poured into old wineskins. There must first be a time to stabilize the beachhead and secure territory in the new land, as in the believer's new life.

Broadly, the six major events of these two chapters, embracing a period of only a few days in Gilgal, may be divided into two general categories: remembering what has gone on in the past and beginning the experiences of a new future. Let us rearrange sequentially, from the perspective of the believer's life, the events at Gilgal. The first command of God is to

1. *Remember the Cross*. To the Jew it is remember the Passover. To the believer it is remember the cross. Central to Jewish history is the unalterable truth that deliverance from Egyptian bondage was afforded at the price of great effort. There was death in the shedding of blood, faith in the blood that was shed, and judgment on those apart from the blood. It was not without the force of both a great tragedy and a great sacrifice that deliverance from bondage was secured. It was

basic to the Hebrew religion and must forever be memorialized. Just so is the cross pictured in the Passover both basic and central to the believer's possession and victory in Christ.

In Galatians 2:20, Paul reminds us that the life we are now living in this flesh we live by the faith *of* the Son of God who gave himself for us. This physical, fleshly life is lived out by the faith of the Son of God who died for us. Paul does not say faith *in* the Son of God, but the faith *of* the Son of God. We actually live our human life by him, the life *of* the Son of God. And in what capacity? Not in his healing, teaching, or preaching ministry, but in his redemptive ministry in which he gave himself for us.

The essence of the Christian life, then, always goes back to the cross. There are my roots, and there, my stability. Christ died for me. In the cross of Christ I glory, for Christ now liveth his life in me. For them and for us, then, this essential truth must be eternally memorialized as a visual reminder to our faith.

In chapter 5, verses 10-11, the Passover is kept. This is the first time, to our knowledge, that this generation kept the Passover feast, memorializing their deliverance from bondage by the blood. The only two other Passover observances recorded in the Scriptures to date are in Egypt and Sinai, at the beginning of the wilderness journey.

For forty years the Passover had not been kept, and now this new, young generation, in the full bloom of an ecstatic first great victory at Jordan must memorialize their roots: "When I see the blood, I will pass over you" (Ex. 12:13). Our Lord has as well given the Christian a memorial to the cross. In the bread and cup of the Lord's Supper, "This do," Jesus said, "in remembrance of me" (Luke 22:19).

2. *Remember the Resurrection*. New Testament baptism by immersion, and it is precisely that, is a picture of the

resurrection of Christ—the other side of the cross essential to securing our salvation. Had Christ only died for our sins, we would be yet in our sins. The resurrection validated the efficacy of the cross. For he was crucified for our sins, but rose for our justification. In the cross he purchased our ticket for our trip to heaven. In the resurrection he used the ticket and put us on the plane.

The resurrection of Christ and the believer's faith in the identity with it is memorialized in immersion baptism. Upon emerging through the river of death, resurrected on the other side, the children of Israel were instructed to memorialize their resurrection by the placing of twelve stones as a monument (4:3-8). You will recall that in 3:12 Joshua commanded twelve men out of the tribes to be selected. In context, it appears that they were selected to carry the ark, but the priests were to carry the ark, and they all belonged to one tribe—the tribe of Levi. These men did not carry the ark.

For what purpose were they selected? It is only when we arrive at chapter 4, verses 2-3 that we learn the reason. Every man was to carry a stone from the midst of the Jordan, stacking them together to make a monument to their resurrection, just as baptism memorializes our resurrection with Christ. These stones were to stimulate the children of Israel to their own religious education, creating an atmosphere in which they would ask questions (vv. 6-7).

What a challenge to Christian parents for our lives to be a living monument to the resurrection power of Christ that our children shall ask of our Christian activity, "What mean ye by these stones?"

Interestingly, in verses 1-2 it was only after everyone had passed over that these twelve men went back into the middle of the river (v. 8). They brought their stones up out of the midst of the river on the shores of Gilgal for eternal memorials. In verse

9, however, much speculation has surrounded the issue of Joshua setting up twelve stones in the midst of Jordan. It is quite possible that actually two monuments were erected—one at God's direction on the shore, and one at Joshua's own bidding in the midst of Jordan. We do not know that God told him specifically to do so, nor is it necessary to record whether he did so or not, but Joshua acted within the scope of God's will and the freedom that was his as a believer in memorializing the grace and power of God even further.

The expression that the stones are there to this day means that they were there years later when the book was written. Perhaps in the fall and spring as the waters rose and fell they would emerge again year after year as a constant reminder to those who passed by that they not only came out of the river, but had actually stood in the midst of the river. Surely we, as well, could never do too much to memorialize with our gifts, our efforts, and our buildings, the greatness of God in our lives.

3. *Remember the Covenant.* Chapter 5, verses 2-9, tells us that the rite of circumcision, again for the first time with this generation, was reestablished. Circumcision was an external sign of the covenant relationship of these people with God. Because they were born Jews did not necessarily mean that their sins were automatically forgiven and heaven was ensured. They had to repent personally and have faith in God as anyone does who comes to Christ.

What does it mean that they are the chosen people? Chosen to be what? The Jews were chosen by God to be the human instrumentality through which the gospel would come into the world. It was a privilege that they chose to reject, and one that was then given to the Gentiles. But that was God's permissive will, not his perfect will. The prophets were Jewish. The authors of the Bible, except one, Luke, were Jewish. Jesus was

Jewish. The land was Jewish, as were the disciples. They were in covenant relationship with him to bring the Messiah into the world and the message of God's saving grace. And circumcision was an external sign of that covenant relationship.

But that was the ministry of the Hebrews as a people. Each must personally repent of his or her sins and turn to God in faith. Circumcision did not take them to heaven any more than baptism takes us to heaven. The true baptism is of the heart, where we die to self and live again unto him.

These things are important, but they are important only as symbols of a covenant relationship, and not actually a part of the relationship itself. The past, then, and the present must be memorialized by the Passover, by the stones, and by circumcision. And what of the future? What of the new?

4. *They Will Be Fed in a New Way* (5:11-12). Once in the land they began to "eat of the old corn." One is immediately impressed that the writer states that it was *old* corn. It is as though our Lord were saying to them, "This corn has been here waiting for you a long time. Where have you been?" This land had belonged to them for forty years, but through sin and unbelief they failed to know experientially what was theirs positionally. A beautiful new gospel hymn reminds us that, "he was there all the time." How oft does our Lord say to the wanderer, "Welcome home. I've been waiting for you. I was here all the time. Everything was ready. It's always been ready, and where were you?"

But now in their beloved land of Canaan, the Lord would deal with them in a new way. For immediately the miraculous provision of God to meet their physical need by daily supply of fresh manna from heaven ceased. The wilderness experience was a time of transition. Like the apostolic age it was necessary for God to deal with them on a miraculous basis. But we must not look for the miraculous when the ordinary will suffice. Ordinary conditions are best, and it is a sign of our maturity to learn that. How often do I hear people say, "I wish we could return to the apostolic age." But who wants to go back to the wilderness? Miracles validated spoken words in the apostolic age. God still performs miracles today, but now we have his Word and it validates itself.

The sensational was fine in the wilderness, but now they had grown up and reached maturity, and God would meet their needs in a quite ordinary day-to-day way as they planted and cultivated and harvested the land.

5. *There Is a New Awareness of God's Presence.* In the past God was Provider and Guide when they needed food and direction, but now they were in a land of battle and they needed a captain. So God, who always is to us what we need when we need him, came to them in a new way as "captain of the host of the Lord" (5:13-15).

There is a time to quit feasting on the land and go out and conquer the enemy of the land. The Christian must move beyond celebration to conflict. The real world is out there and Satan is its lord. In verse 13 of chapter 5 "Joshua was by Jericho," looking at the city, and perhaps making his plans. The people remained at Gilgal, and their leader, under the cover of night perhaps, went apart from them to scope out the city of Jericho. Before him, a walled city which Moses' spies had said, "[Reach] up to heaven" (Deut. 1:28). Behind him were two million Israelites depending on his leadership. Now there was no Moses to direct and counsel him. Now it was Joshua and God.

Perhaps he had begun to make a mental list: so many battering rams would be needed, so many soldiers—but wait! Suddenly there appeared before him a man with sword drawn in his hand of whom Joshua inquired, "Are you for us or our enemies?" "No," the man responded. "My service is to the

Lord. As captain of his hosts I am come" (Author, 5:13-14). The implication is that if I fight for you it will be because you fight for my Lord, for my first allegiance is to him.

Who was this captain of the Lord's hosts who came to fight? Hebrews 2:9-10 tells us that Jesus is the captain of our salvation. This may well have been a preincarnate appearance of our Lord Jesus himself. The invisible hosts of God are always about us—standing with us, fighting for us. God showed Elijah 7,000 invisible allies who had not bowed their knees to Baal, and Jesus said before the cross, "Know ye not that I could call down twelve legions of angels and they would come and fight for me?" (Author, Matt. 26:53).

All throughout chapter 5 the Lord has been speaking. Now the captain of the Lord's hosts spoke and in the beginning of chapter 6, the Lord is speaking again. The two expressions appear to be used interchangeably. Perhaps he who commands the Lord's hosts is none other than the Lord himself.

6. *Unfortunately, the Heathen Did Not Remember.* Chapter 5, verse 1, tells us that when all the heathen around the Jordan heard and saw what had happened, their hearts melted within them. The purpose of sixty miles of dry riverbed was then, indeed, for their benefit. The last two verses of chapter 4 make it clear that the purpose of the miracle was "that all the people of the earth might know the hand of the Lord . . . that ye might fear the Lord your God for ever."

Yes, the judgment and power of God are intended to strike fear into the hearts of the unbeliever, but the purpose of the fear and conviction is to stimulate us toward repentance and conversion. It was and remains the only intent of the heart of God with the heathen to convict and save them. How sad it is that conviction does not always bring conversion. The rich young ruler was stirred, but went away lost. Felix trembled, but waited for a more convenient season and was not heard from again.

Oh, how my heart yearns to tell you that the children of Israel never strayed from God and never turned back from these amazing experiences memorialized at Gilgal. But the sad truth is, that not only did not the heathen remember, but neither did the Israelites remember.

> And Joshua the son of Nun, the servant of the Lord, died, being an hundred and ten years old. And they buried him in the border of his inheritance in Timnathheres, in the mount of Ephraim, on the north side of the hill Gaash. And also all that generation were gathered unto their fathers: and there arose another generation after them, which knew not the Lord, nor yet the works which he had done for Israel. And the children of Israel did evil in the sight of the Lord, and served Baalim: And they forsook the Lord God of their fathers, which brought them out of the land of Egypt, and followed other gods, of the gods of the people that were round about them, and bowed themselves unto them, and provoked the Lord to anger. And they forsook the Lord, and served Baal and Ashtaroth (Judg. 2:8-13).

How tragic. They did not live up to what they were memorializing. Their walk did not match their talk. Their actions were not consistent with their profession. The actions of their lives were not consistent with the profession of their lips. And even their own children, the very next generation, went into paganism. It may well be stated that at any given time we are only one generation away from paganism. May God help us not to fail. And the key to victory? Trust and obey!

5
The Walls Came Tumbling Down

Joshua 6:1-27

Within an hour's march of Gilgal was the first major obstacle to the complete conquest of Canaan. It was a critical test, since it was the first one in the new land. As Christians, we continue to be faced with the problems of the old life. These problems are often our Lord's way of bringing before us the major remaining obstacle left from the past. The first thing is often the most important, that with which we must deal repeatedly. After we have been defeated and almost utterly annihilated, spectacular victory may then be ours.

"Jericho was straitly shut up" (v. 1) before the children of Israel. The walls were high; the gates closed immediately and completely. No one went out and no one came in. It is to be remembered that these same people had seen the hand of God and had closed themselves in against his power. What a mighty picture it is of the unpardonable sin, the state in which the unbeliever has so long resisted the tug of the Spirit's call that he has hardened his heart and no longer possesses the capacity to repent.

Undoubtedly, the witness of Rahab had fallen on deaf ears. One must wonder whether the inhabitants of Jericho truly believed that locking all the gates would cause them to stand before God against whose power the gates of hell will never prevail. The report of the twelve spies had been that the gates reached as high as the heavens. Still, how foolish for any person to think that he could close himself in against God.

The Lord said to Joshua, "See, I have given Jericho into your hand" (v. 2). Positionally Jericho was not theirs, but if they could only see it with the eye of faith, it was theirs for the taking. Faith may, indeed, see things which are hidden to mere human sight and reason, but the condition is that there be no reliance on human effort. The announcement is, "See, I have given Jericho to you." It is God's victory, but ours to accomplish with the eye of faith.

Immediately thereupon, though, God had said, "I have given you the land." He now added, "Ye shall compass the city." His heavenly promise does not make void human responsibility. We are to act as willing participants with God in our work on earth. The gospel will be preached as a witness to all nations, but it is we who are to go.

Verses 4-6 must surely have sounded strange to the ears of Joshua and the people. The organization was to be as follows: The army of approximately one-half million men would lead the way, followed by seven trumpeters, followed by the ark with the congregation in the rear. For seven days they would compass the city, blowing the rams' horns, and on the seventh day make seven trips around and shout, but then, and then alone, would the obstacle fall down before them.

How foolish a plan it must have seemed to Joshua, but our Lord has "chosen the foolish things of the world to confound the wise; . . . and things which are not, to bring to nought the things that are" (1Cor. 1:27-28). It usually seems to be his way to set aside the prestigious, the famous, the rich, and use the poor, despicable, and unlikely. And why? That in all things he might have the preeminence, for he will share his glory with no one.

Four sevens are listed in this passage: seven priests, seven trumpets, seven days, and seven times. The number seven is the biblical number for completion. In six days our Lord created the heavens and the earth. He rested on the seventh in honor of his completed work. God was saying that the victory at Jericho would be complete and be completely his. There is no failure when he is in control.

The seven trumpets were not the lyrical silver trumpets of the Year of Jubilee, but were rams' horns making a low, earthy, guttural sound. The commonness of men represented in the horns and the glory of God represented in the ark would work hand in hand to bring about the victory. The trumpets remind us of John the Baptist who trumpeted the sound of the coming of the Lamb of God, as well as the trumpet of God which shall join with the shout and the voice of the archangel when Christ returns in glory.

The people were to give a tumultuous shout. A careful reading of 1 Thessalonians 4:13-18 will make it clear that in Christ's coming for his own, three things will happen from the heavens: the trumpet of God will sound, the voice of the archangel will ring out, and there will be a shout. That shout is not from the archangel. He only speaks with his voice. That shout may well be, as was this shout, the shout of the people in victory as God brings with him those who have died believing in Jesus Christ and who now live with him and return with him.

One can imagine the consternation of the city's inhabitants as the people of God walked about blowing the horns. The citizens of Jericho waited in dread to see what the God who had parted the Jordan was up to now with his people.

Oh, Christian, never forget that the devil trembles within that fortified wall that stands before you, that impregnable Jericho of your life, if you will only obey, believe, and shout the victory that is yours in Christ.

In verse 5 God instructed the people to shout only when they heard the trumpet sound, and not before. Verse 10 augments that instruction to say that during the seven-day journey there was to be no sound by the people at all—no talking, no singing, no whispering—until God gave the command. They were to save up all their vocal effort for one final shout. With dynamic faith there must also be discipline. It may not be time to shout victory yet, but you and I know in our hearts that the day of victory comes soon.

Remember again the picture. First the army led the way, undoubtedly by the captain of the Lord's hosts. They were surely a marching army of faith as are we who follow our heavenly Joshua, the Lord Jesus.

One day they went around, and two and three, and daily until the sixth day Joshua arose early to arrange the army, the trumpets, the priests, and the rereward (rear ward, or gathering host) in order. Just as our Lord arose early in the morning to pray, we may be sure that when we who follow him step into the battles and trials of each day, he has been there before. Yet, what patience that must have followed. Consistently, day after day, with unwavering allegiance and obedience to him in whom they had absolute faith. Never forget that obedience and faith are the two keys to victory.

It is hard to imagine the anticipation and expectancy that must have grown in their hearts. But thank God again for these stirring words, "And it came to pass" (v. 15). For on the seventh day they went around seven times. Once a day for six days, and seven times on the seventh, thirteen trips around

Jericho, a city of probably one-half million, the journey to have taken many long hours the last day. Why thirteen trips? It was not for God's benefit, but for theirs. God knew that it would take that long for them to realize they could not do it themselves. There is absolutely no way that human effort can bring down the walls of the impossible Jerichos of our lives. It is his to give and ours to believe and receive in obedience; and when we learn that lesson, whether it be thirteen days or thirteen years, victory will be ours, as well.

From verse 16, move directly to verse 20, and see that as the people shouted, God was faithful and the walls fell down flat. Between verses 16 and 20 there are parentheses in verses 17 to 19. Here our Lord told them the first of two sets of instructions. In the city there were two things— people and possessions. This first parenthetical directive deals with the possessions. The accursed things must not be taken. They must be destroyed completely. Deuteronomy 7:25-26 says, "The graven images of their gods shall ye burn with fire: thou shalt not desire the silver or gold that is on them, nor take it unto thee, lest thou be snared therein: for it is an abomination to the Lord thy God. Neither shalt thou bring an abomination into thine house, lest thou be a cursed thing like it: but thou shalt utterly detest it, and thou shalt utterly abhor it; for it is a cursed thing." The accursed thing, then, was the silver, gold, and gems that were on the heathen gods and dedicated to pagan deities. They were not to be taken.

However, the valuable vessels that are not accursed may be taken, and are to be consecrated to the Lord's treasury. The principle, then, is this: Everything that has to do with evil must go, and everything else goes to God. On some future occasions they would be allowed to sack the city and keep certain spoils, but each time they must be careful to precisely obey God's command.

Herein is the law of the firstfruits: Jericho was different; it was the first victory, and the spoils must go to God. He will have the firstfruits of the harvest, the first tithe of the possession, the first day of the week, and first place in our lives.

But within the city there were more important things than possessions. There were evil people, too. They were evil people serving evil gods, and they would keep the children of Israel from Jehovah. They would have to be slain by the sword to the last person and animal. Complete annihilation of all living, evil things. You must sever from your Christian life relationships from the old life with evil companions and evil possessions. Verse 21 states that they are to be destroyed with the sword. The sword is usually a picture of the Word of God.

In verse 24 all that remained in the city was to be burned with fire. The primary picture of fire in the Scripture is judgment, and the secondary picture is the Holy Spirit. The Spirit, then, and the sword must join together to bring the judgment of death to every vestige of the old and evil.

Ephesians, as the New Testament commentary on Joshua, tells us to "Take . . . the sword of the Spirit, which is the word of God' (6:17). The Holy Spirit of Christ, the invisible presence of our heavenly Joshua among us, will fight our battle for us, but the sword of the Spirit is the Word, and it is ours to place within his hands a sword with which to fight. We must read, memorize, quote, assimilate, stand on, and practice the Word of God if we are to place within the hand of the Spirit a sword with which to fight our battles, destroy our Jerichos, and defeat our foes.

It is interesting to note that before the judgment began God, confirming the word of the two spies who had spoken for him within his authority and his will, allowed them to bring Rahab and her family out to safety. Verse 23 adds, "And all that she had." Joshua knew that this great woman would have nothing of her house dedicated to idols. No qualifications here, no exception needed for Rahab. She was God's woman, all that she had was godly—bring it all with her.

Verse 26 records a curse pronounced by Joshua on any man who attempted to rebuild that city. Our Lord is doubly displeased with those who would corrupt the life of the believer, enticing him, supporting him in rebuilding the old Jerichos of the former life, once so important and now destroyed by the sword and the Spirit. The curse stated specifically that any man who would do so would accomplish the feat at the cost of the lives of his firstborn child and youngest son.

First Kings 16:34 records that is precisely what happened when Hiel the Bethelite rebuilt Jericho and buried his firstborn, Abiram, and youngest son, Segub, in the foundation of the city. Believing in reincarnation, it was common for pagan rulers to attempt to perpetuate their presence in mammoth monuments to themselves by burying their children alive in their foundations. It is believed that Hiel precisely followed that heathen custom.

The chapter closes with a beautiful addendum that "the Lord was with Joshua; and his fame was noised throughout all the country" (v. 27). It may well be said that the Lord was with Joshua because Joshua was with the Lord, and that our Lord is pleased to make famous those who serve him as faithfully as did the son of Nun.

6
The Lull
After the Storm

Joshua 7:1-26

Many are familiar with Edward Gibbon's famous book, *The Decline and Fall of the Roman Empire*. And many have heard of *The Rise and Fall of the Third Reich*. But thank God the story of the Christian, though one may stumble, may always be "The Fall and Rise of the Believer."

Chapters 7 and 8 form a unit openly telling the story of the people of God falling flat on their faces immediately following their monumental victory at Jericho. But to the praise of the dear Lord, there is immediately the story of their restitution. The believer need never stay on his face. Though we stumble, we can rise again. Christ is our victory.

Chapter 7 presents the steps to Israel's defeat, and chapter 8, the story of renewed victory. Together they form a unit of truth that is essential to the Christian life. It is a simple, but important, story, from which we may learn the steps which lead to defeat and those which lead us to victory.

It is precisely this pattern of honesty which leads us, in part, to the conviction that the Bible is, without any doubt, the Word of God. Many books attempt to hide the failures of their heroes, but the Word of God is open and honest in its presentation of the sins, as well as the successes, of the saints.

Fresh from the bloom of victory at Jericho it would be wonderful if chapter 7 began with the word *and*. ("And they continued to grow in the Lord, going from victory to victory.") The truth is, however, that it begins with the word *but*. The story is an unpleasant one, and the reason is in verse 1, "But the children of Israel committed a trespass [against the Lord]."

Immediately thereupon we discover that Achan, one seemingly insignificant member of the tribe of Judah, had disobeyed the Lord and taken of the "accursed thing," a valuable piece of goods dedicated to idols and forbidden among the spoils of Jericho. We are immediately confronted with the awesome truth that though only one person had sinned, God dealt with them en masse. "The children of Israel" committed the trespass. God was dealing with them as a people at this juncture in history, and would emphasize for all time that his people rise and fall together.

Sin does affect others; in the home, in business, in the church, and in the nation. We do not live to ourselves, and we do not die to ourselves. Whether we live or die, what we do affects others.

In the first verse the plot is laid which undergirds the whole story. The problem—secret sin in the camp. In verses 2-6 spies are again sent to check out their objective. The report was that Ai was insignificant and ill-armed. It was nothing for them. They could handle it themselves. Only two to three thousand troops would be necessary this time. Nothing at all like the half-million-member army that led the march around Jericho. But horror of horrors, the people of God were routed by the men of Ai and scattered in a humiliating and total defeat.

Joshua fell on his face and tore his clothes in horror and dismay before the Lord.

Let us examine the ingredients which led to the defeat of these believers.

1. **There was an obvious case of self-sufficiency.** The people viewed Ai as an insignificant enemy, well within their ability to handle. True, the hand of God was needed at mighty Jericho, but, after all, could they not handle Ai by themselves? This attitude becomes obvious at the report of the spies, "Let not all the people go up, but let about two or three thousand men go up and smite Ai" (v. 3). From mere human logic this seems to be a good plan. A half-million troops to match a half-million-man army in Jericho, but two or three thousand to battle the troops at Ai. That was good thinking, if only human effort were needed to win the victory. But how quickly they had forgotten—the troops at Jericho had nothing to do with the victory at Jericho. It was not a human effort, but a divine victory.

We make a grave mistake when we look to our Lord only for the difficult problems of life, and when the victory comes, forget too quickly that the victory was the Lord's. "Surely," we think, "we have handled the big problems. We can handle the little problems." But the truth is we can handle neither. It takes no more of God's power to heal cancer than a cold. It simply takes God's power. It takes no more of God's grace to save the hardened criminal, and no less for the youngest child. It just takes his grace.

Never let it be forgotten that "the battle is the Lord's." An obvious case of self-sufficiency and pride over a victory that had been won not in their own power, but in the Lord's, was the initial step to the defeat at insignificant Ai.

2. **There was an apparent abundance of prayerlessness.**

It is characteristic of self-sufficiency to make one's own decisions. We, in effect, become our own god and depend on our own logic and human reason when we exaggerate the importance of ourselves.

The victory at Jericho was the Lord's. How quickly they seemed to forget. "We did it, and we shall do it again," was probably their cry. Why pray? Why ask God's direction at all? There is no hint of dependence on God at Ai, no prayer, no counsel, no direction, but mere human wisdom alone. "Big obstacle, big army; small obstacle, small army," was their logic. No need to ask God. They had it all figured out. But what a tragic mistake it was to ignore the Captain of the invisible host.

Immediately upon their defeat (v. 6), Joshua fell on his face and pleaded with the Lord. Joshua's prayer was just a little late. Had he sought the Lord on his face for guidance, he would not have been on his face in sackcloth and ashes. While God's plan for Jericho was seven days of marching, his plan for Ai was an ambush. The issue is not whether ambushes or marches are more effective in conquering cities, but whether or not God is allowed to be God.

God had a plan, God had a will, and failure to consult God for his perfect plan was devastating to Joshua and the children of Israel. One hundred victories in our lives may never assure the one hundred and first. God is to be consulted and his direction sought at every juncture of life. He who creates no two snowflakes alike has a perfect and special plan for each individual. How tragic to ignore his will and lean upon our own understanding.

3. **Disobedience leads to defeat.** It is always the case— "When lust hath conceived, it bringeth forth sin: and sin, when it is finished, bringeth forth death" (Jas. 1:15). In verse 11 God informs Joshua that the reason for Israel's failure was her

sin. "Israel hath sinned," and "neither will I be with you any more, except ye destroy the accursed thing from among you" (v. 12) is the resolute demand of God.

God had clearly said that no accursed thing, no valuable possession dedicated to idols, was to be taken from Jericho and kept by the people. There was no need for translation of the will of God here, no call to interpret what he meant. The direction was clear and precise. "Nothing valuable from Jericho for yourselves." That which was dedicated to heathen gods was to be destroyed, and the valuable things undedicated were to be brought into the treasury of the Lord. But in neither case could anything be kept.

Achan, along with the entire congregation, knew precisely the will of God. Disobedience, not ignorance, was the problem. When finally confronted with his guilt, Achan's admission was made with a careful explanation of why. In verse 21 a perfect analysis of sin is recorded.

1. "I saw . . . [the beautiful possession]";
2. "I coveted them"; and
3. "[I] took them."

This is always the downward progression from the lust of the eye to the wages of sin—death. There are three steps which lead us from temptation to evil. The lust of the eye, the lust of the flesh, and the pride of life. Achan said, "I lusted with my eye." It is the first step to evil to live a life that is materialistically oriented, to want everything one sees; an insatiable desire in the lusts of the flesh follows, and we will not be satisfied until we have what we see. Regardless of whose it is, regardless of the consequential or the sacred boundaries around it, the first two steps toward evil are always the lust of the eye and the lust of the flesh—"I saw . . . then I coveted."

The end result is always the same—"[I] took." The pride of life which dictates, "What is important is what pleases *me*. *I* took it because *I* wanted it for *me*. It pleased *me* to have it, and the law and prohibition of God make no difference." That is the pride of life. In other words, "What is *my* god is what pleases *me*. What *I* do is what *I* want. *My* world revolves around *my* personal pleasure. *I* saw, *I* coveted, *I* took."

The chapter closes with the plaintive plea of Joshua. "Why hast thou troubled us?" (v. 25). We do not sin in isolation. Tragedy of tragedies—thirty-six men were killed in a useless defeat (v. 5). The people of God were dispirited and their leader brokenhearted because one man was unfaithful to the command of God: "[Thou shalt not touch] the accursed thing" (6:18).

The steps toward death are always the same. Self-sufficiency leads to independence from God, and independence leads to disobedience. The wages of sin are still death.

Oh, believer, stay close to him who is your sufficiency. No man is an island. The smallest package in the world is a man wrapped up in himself. We need our Lord, his direction, his grace, and his power afresh each morning.

Had the victors at Jericho been humbly grateful, they would have been on their knees thanking God and seeking his direction for Ai. It is a lesson that we must learn well if we would stand among even the smaller tests of life which can defeat us so greatly.

7
The Comeback Trail

Joshua 8:1-35

Thank the Lord that those wonderful words, "and it came to pass" (v. 14), greet us again and again after the Ai's of our life. It is not characteristic of our Lord to leave us fallen on our faces. The great encourager told Joshua to "Get thee up; wherefore liest thou thus upon thy face?" (7:10). "Down, but not out" is always the glorious position of those who cry to the Lord and hear his faithful, "Get thee up."

The eighth chapter is the story of the comeback from defeat at Ai, and it is one filled with example and truth for the believer. We have seen the steps that lead to defeat: self-sufficiency, prayerlessness, and disobedience. Let us trace the steps that led again to victory. For a moment we shall dip again into the seventh chapter and see the beginnings of the journey upward.

1. **Acknowledgment of Guilt and Confession.** It is surprising to note that the Lord demanded a tribe-by-tribe, family-by-family, house-by-house, and man-by-man search until the guilty party was found. I want to raise the question as to why

the Lord did not point out Achan immediately as the offender, as with the case of Nathan's confrontation with David. There are two possibilities, I think, that merit our attention.

First, God was making a dramatic presentation of truth to these people for all time that sin cannot be hidden, sin affects everybody, and that God means precisely what he says. Early in the foundation of the people of God, the Lord dealt stringently with their sins. The same is true in the apostolic era when, in the early church, Ananias and Sapphira lied and were stricken dead by the Holy Ghost. Our Lord was attempting to nail down some standards—to dramatically teach that he means what he says and says what he means. "These things happened for an example to us who believe."

Secondly, I firmly believe that God was dealing graciously with Achan by giving him every chance to repent. With each acknowledgment of innocence, the finger of judgment came one step closer to Achan. How many hundreds of people were declared guiltless before Achan's guilt was determined? At any juncture he could have cried out, "I have sinned. May God be merciful." By every biblical precedent we believe that God would have been merciful and forgiving. Confronted with the truth, David was quick to confess, "I have sinned" (Ps. 41:4). Our Lord was pleased to say of him, "[He is] a man after mine own heart" (Acts 13:22, cf. 1 Sam. 13:14).

But the verdict upon Achan: "And all Israel stoned him with stones" (v. 25). The reason? Achan's confession was a forced confession. He rejected opportunity after opportunity to repent. He spurned the grace of God and hardened his heart until at last his opportunity was gone. If Achan's sin meant lost blessing to the entire congregation, his judgment visited loss of life on his own family. Chapter 7:24-25 tells us that his sons, daughters, cattle, possessions, and stolen goods were brought before the people of Israel. Cattle and family members were slain and all possessions burned. God would have the people know that idolatry and disobedience are serious issues.

Please note that the command of Joshua (7:19) is "Give . . . glory to the Lord . . . God and make confession." Both a willing confession and a forced confession give glory to God. The Philippian writer declared "Every knee should bow, . . . and that every tongue confess that Jesus Christ is Lord, to the glory of the Father" (vv. 10-11). If you willingly confess him now, it will be a confession unto salvation. Your forced acknowledgment of the lordship of Christ will be a confession unto damnation.

Achan's forced confession did not save him from the wrath of God and death, nor will your forced confession of Christ as Lord save you from God's judgment. But one way or the other you will bow the knee and you will confess that Christ is Lord. If you are lost, I pray that you do not follow the example of Achan. Confess him willingly now. "For whosoever therefore shall confess me before men, him will I confess before my Father which is in heaven" (Matt. 10:32).

2. **Faith in God's Promise to Restore.** "Fear not, . . . I have given into thy hand the king of Ai, and his people and his city and his land" (8:1). Confession had brought about immediate restitution of fellowship, and the praising of God was perpetuated. Everything was just like it was before. Everything was all right. Our Lord is ready to forgive. Confession alone is all that is needed. "If we confess our sins, he is faithful and just to forgive us our sins, and to cleanse us from all unrighteousness" (1 John 1:9). Cleansing, fellowship, perfect relationship, and righteous standing are the promises of God to all who confess.

3. **Obedience to Direction.** From verse 2 to the end of the chapter, we find the people of God carrying out Jehovah's simple plan to capture Ai. The people were to be divided into

three groups. Some were to wait in ambush for the people of Ai. Some were to feign an aborted attack on the city, leading the pursuers of Ai into the ambush, and some were to remain behind to set the city afire when the inhabitants pursued Israel. The plan worked perfectly. As they faced the Israelites again, they looked back to their city to see it in flames. Turning again toward Ai, they were caught in a trap between the captors of the city and the "liers in wait" (v. 13) in ambush. The rout of the enemy was complete, the king was taken alive and hanged in ridicule and shame on a tree (v. 29). This time human insufficiency had been acknowledged, God had been sought, his will perfectly executed, and the victory was complete.

4. **Every Resource Must Be Brought into the Effort.** You will notice in verse 11 that all the people were used in the effort—some in ambush, some pretending defeat, and some burning the city. All appear to have participated (v. 21). Nothing was left outside the control of Almighty God.

Dear Christian reader, you will never know victory in the smallest Ai of your life, let alone the overwhelming Jerichos, until all you are is brought under control of his lordship. No halfhearted effort will gain the desired victory.

Notice in verse 16 that "all the people that were in Ai were called together to pursue after them." The devil throws everything he has into the fray, and the people of God can do no less. In verse 17 the nearby city of Bethel joined with the men of Ai to unanimously go after Israel. The devil always has his collusion with the world, his allies in evil. Everything that he has and everything that he is he thrusts into the battle against our Lord for his kingdom.

Tomorrow would be too late. This was the day of battle. It was all or nothing at all. The people of God understood, rallied, and won. Nothing but our best effort as individuals and as the people of God is sufficient for this hour. What an important time in world history to be alive! Sewers of sin overrun the waters of society. It is time for all-out war on evil and total commitment to world evangelism. Let us be at our best; all of us. And all that we have is required. The devil is throwing everything he has into the battle, and we can be victorious if we will do no less.

We see in verse 29 that an open display was made of the king of Ai who was hanged on a tree until evening. Our Lord made just such an open display of our enemy at the cross.

> And you, being dead in your sins and the uncircumcision of your flesh, hath he quickened together with him, having forgiven you all trespasses; Blotting out the handwriting of ordinances that was against us, which was contrary to us, and took it out of the way, nailing it to his cross; And having spoiled principalities and powers, he made a shew of them openly, triumphing over them in it (Col. 2:13-15).

5. **A Firm New Commitment to Absolute Obedience Is Required.** Following an offering of gratitude to the Lord (vv. 30-31), Joshua meticulously led the people into a recommitment to absolute obedience to every jot and tittle of Moses' Law. We are not sure whether the Ten Commandments, the sayings of Moses to Israel, or the entire first five books of the Bible are referred to, but Joshua dramatically led his people in restating their obedience to "the law of Moses" (v. 32).

The Law was written upon an altar of stone (v. 32) in the presence of all the people. Thereupon (v. 33), the people were divided, as Moses had done, into two groups, half on Mount Gerizim, half on Mount Ebal. For endless hours half the people recited the cursings of the Law to those who disobey, followed by resounding "Amen." On the other side of the valley, those on the other mountain responded with a united recitation of the blessings of the Law to those who obey. And the entire congregation shouted, "Amen."

Following this, all the law was read by Joshua, and verse 35 is careful to point out that not a word was left out. Everyone heard the Word of God. All of it! This was a significant day in the life of Israel. Vividly behind them lay the memory of the events of a black day in their history. They would learn for time immemorial that God means what he says in his Word, that the law is eternally binding, that sin affects others, and the wages of sin is death.

Chapters 7 and 8 are two classic pictures of the Christian life—the steps which proceed down from God and which build again our fellowship with him. To those who stand in fellowship with him, I say, "Be warned." Self-sufficiency leads to independence; independence to prayerlessness; prayerlessness to disobedience; and disobedience to death.

To those who lie in failure and defeat I say, "Take heart." There is a way out of the wilderness, a road back to God. Confess, believe, obey his will, throw all you have into the effort, and give attention to every detail of his Word. To err is human. To rise, to stand again, is divine.

8
Spiritual Strategy

Joshua 9:1-27

Joshua's ninth chapter is difficult, if not impossible, to exegcte in the accustomed verse-by-verse style. It is best related in story form with references as needed to specific texts. It is, nonetheless, one of the more important chapters in the book. Let us refresh our memory by stating that Joshua is the background which paints a picture of principles in the Christian warfare augmented and enlarged in Paul's Letter to the Ephesians. Each battle and each obstacle throws a little different light on the many-faceted aspects of the believer's warfare with the evil one. We will recall that the lesson at Jericho was to trust God and be obedient regardless of external appearances. It was a lesson in the changeless truth that victory only comes on the exclusive basis of absolute trust in God's sufficiency and in the resultant obedience of our faith.

At Ai the lessons were different. Sin must be exposed. That which was dedicated to the devil may never be brought into the service of God. Obedience to the minutest detail of his command is imperative. The sin of one affects the many. We are a family, and we rise and fall together. Before the conflict with the confederation of Canaanite kings (v. 10) there is a lesson to be learned about the deception of the enemy who deceivingly twists the Word and destroys from within (ch. 9).

Following the victory at Ai, a confederation of kings from six different kingdoms joined together to plot against Israel (v. 1). It is logical from human perspective that they joined together, believing Israel could be defeated only by massive military power. When the numbers were smaller at Ai, Israel was defeated. When they were large, Israel was victorious. The key to victory over Israel? Force must be matched with force. A large army of six united kingdoms was the answer. But what they did not know is that neither the victory at Jericho nor Ai had anything to do with numbers, but with the power of God and obedience to his revealed will.

The chapter begins by saying "And it came to pass." Following the victory at Ai, there was a period of time during which Joshua and the Israelites had opportunity to regroup and bask in the delight of victory over the past, and meditate on the future. During this time the brilliant military strategist, Joshua, made a plan to make a wedge toward the heart of Canaan westward from Ai, dividing the country into two parts; then conquering first, the south, and then the north. It is good to withdraw to a time of meditation and planning following victory, as well as defeat. The battles of life must be well-thought-out in advance during the early, quiet hours of the day. But do not be surprised that Satan is planning, too. We have learned that lesson at Ai. When all of the people of Israel went up against Ai, all of Ai came out to meet them. The devil throws everything he has into the battle when God's people are serious and when they are victorious. You may always expect an all-out frontal attack by the evil one following periods of great victory. The six kings of the coast agreed to attempt together what could never be done alone.

You will remember our Lord's story of a solitary evil spirit driven from a man, only to find that he returned to his heart, bringing with him seven other evil spirits. What the devil cannot do alone, he will attempt to do by rallying his forces, but he does not take defeat lightly and he will never give up. At some point during the planning meeting of the six kings, the inhabitants of Gibeon appeared to withdraw from the original plan of a united frontal attack and came to the conclusion that they would deal with Israel on their own and in a different way (vv. 3-4). There were two reasons for this independent course of action: (1) The men of Gibeon who withdrew had a different form of government. They were ruled by elders rather than by a single king (v. 11), and they had to make an independent decision. (2) As we shall see, they were obviously party to additional information other than that known by the other five kings, and the decision at which the elders arrived was a different one.

You will note, incidentally, that this independent group which took a different course of action was referred to interchangeably as the Gibeonites and the Hivites. The Hivite kingdom was in Canaan (v. 1). Gibeon was one of four cities there (v. 16-17) and was, in fact, the greatest of the four (10:2). The greatness of the city of Gibeon was such that its influence obviously overshadowed the entire Hivite kingdom, whose citizens came to be known interchangeably as Hivites and Gibeonites (vv. 1, 3, 7, 17).

Before we attempt to learn how the Gibeonites or Hivites came to arrive at their unusual course of action, it is necessary for us to first understand precisely what it was they decided to do. The writer of the Book of Joshua states, "they did work wilily" (v. 4). That is to say, they arrived at a crafty plan by which to deceive Israel rather than fight her. Their plan (vv. 4-6) was to appear to have traveled a long distance, having just arrived at the camp of the Israelites from a country far outside of Canaan. Thereupon, they offered to make a league with Israel. Joshua was troubled and uncertain at their offer (vv. 7-8), but agreed to the league, nonetheless (v. 15). Why would the Gibeonites-Hivites go to such great extremes to appear to have come from a far country to make a league with the Israelites? The key to understanding the ninth chapter is the last two words of verse 1, "heard thereof."

You will recall that following the victory at Ai, Joshua was so intent upon the people learning the lesson of obedience to the word of God taught at Ai that he commanded all of the people to divide into two camps and recite the law. I believe that Joshua followed Moses' procedures as seen in Deuteronomy. There, upon Mt. Ebal and Mt. Gerizim, hour after hour the people spoke back and forth to each other all of the blessings and the cursings of the law that Moses had commanded Joshua to lead the people to recite once inside Canaan. Joshua had decided in his heart, "Now is the time for the dramatic recitation of the Word of God." Israel must never forget all that God had spoken. This recitation came at the end of chapter 8, and is immediately followed by the opening verse of chapter 9, which states that the six kings had *heard thereof.* Perhaps only the Hivites had heard clearly. Perhaps only they had heard it all, or they were the only ones to understand what was said. But the Hivites had heard God's Word. Do not forget that they represent the deception of the evil one and they are pictured as overhearing—being aware of, knowing, and twisting to deceive us with "all the Word of God." Remember, the lesson to be learned in chapter 9 is that Satan knows the Word of God and knows how to twist it to his own purpose, and that purpose is to deceive the believer.

And what was the word that they overheard that caused them to pretend as though they had come from afar? The answer to that lies in Deuteronomy 20:10-17:

> When thou comest nigh unto a city to fight against it, then proclaim peace unto it. And it shall be, if it make thee answer of peace, and open unto thee, then it shall be, that all the people that is found therein shall be tributaries unto thee, and they shall serve thee. And if it will make no peace with thee, but will make war against thee, then thou shalt besiege it: And when the Lord thy God hath delivered it into thine hands, thou shalt smite every male thereof with the edge of the sword: But the women, and the little ones, and the cattle, and all that is in the city, even all the spoil thereof, shalt thou take unto thyself; and thou shalt eat the spoil of thine enemies, which the Lord thy God hath given thee. Thus shalt thou do unto all the cities which are very far off from thee, which are not of the cities of these nations. But of the cities of these people, which the Lord thy God doth give thee for an inheritance, thou shalt save alive nothing that breatheth: But thou shalt utterly destroy them; namely, the Hittites, and the Amorites, the Canaanites, and the Perizzites, the Hivites, and the Jebusites; as the Lord thy God hath commanded thee.

Moses was commanding the people in the law of warfare. This law is a part of "all the words of the law" Moses commanded Joshua to direct the people to recite to each other once inside of Canaan (8:34). And it is *this* portion of the law which the Gibeonites overheard and caused them to act as they do. God had commanded Moses to instruct Joshua that on the journey to the Promised Land (through the wilderness) they were to offer peace and surrender to any city they confronted. This was to be done to the cities which were very far off (in the wilderness) from the cities inside the Promised Land (v. 15). But once inside Canaan, the cities God gave them for an inheritance (v. 9), were to be utterly destroyed, allowing nothing that breathed to live.

Among these cities (v. 17) the Hivites were specifically named. Either the other kings did not hear all of the law recited on Ebal and Gerizim, or did not hear it clearly and completely, or they did not understand or believe what they heard. But the Hivites heard and they understood clearly. If they appeared to be from a far country in the wilderness, they could make a league with Israel and live as their servants and tributaries (Deut. 20:11). If, however, they were from the land of Canaan, they were to be killed. The Hivites' answer to the problem? "Though we are from the land of Canaan, we will appear to be from a far country in the wilderness." Mark well that Satan knows the Word of God. He knows how to use it, how to quote it, and how to twist it to deceive us. It is to their regret that they acted this way. The purpose of the Lord in allowing the unbeliever to hear the Word is conversion, and not judgment. Rahab heard what God had done, repented, and was converted. The Hivites heard what God had said and could have been converted, but they chose rather to rebel and to deceive. It is one thing to have accurate knowledge. It is another thing to use that knowledge to make right decisions. Unfortunately, the Gibeonites did not. Notice that there is no question but that they knew the Word well. They were never specific as to the name of the far country from which they came. They were careful not to mention the victories at Ai and Jericho, for they would not have been acquainted with that information had they, indeed, come from afar. The only reference of geography they made was to what God had done in Egypt and to the victories won in the wilderness. Their preparation was thorough, their deception complete. And Joshua, the man of God, was thoroughly deceived.

But do not be deceived when Satan himself comes transformed as an angel of light. Failure is not necessary, and there is no excuse for us to be deceived. We, as Joshua, have ample resources available to us to find and know the truth. Joshua completely ignored three avenues available to him that would have exposed the deception:

1. *He ignored his conscience*. A casual reading of verses 7 and 8 makes it clear that he was unsettled in his heart as to who these people really were and why he should make a league with them. But his skepticism did not lead him to patience. God has given the believer a discerning spirit, and when we are troubled and unsure we should take time to check out the truth. This Joshua did (v. 16), but too late for himself and those for whom he had responsibility. And that resulted in consequences that were both devastating and far-reaching.

2. *He ignored the counsel of the high priest*. God had provided that in matters relating to Israel's national security, the leaders of the people could consult the high priest for specific direction. The Urim and Thummim, a black-and-white stone, were carried in the breastplate of the high priest. When requested by Joshua, he was to seek God's will in prayer, and direction, in turn, would come through the providential selection of one of those two stones. Joshua ignored this specific direction available to him.

3. *He "asked not counsel at the mouth of the Lord" (v. 14)*. God was willing and eager to speak. The syllables were formed in his mouth, and the words "make no league with them" on his lips. But Joshua and his elders did not ask the Lord.

I repeat, there is no excuse for us to be deceived. God has given us good books, good scholars to teach us, the discernment of the Spirit in our hearts, and, above all, his personal answer to prayer. We, like Joshua, must suffer the consequences when we fail to follow God's prescribed course of action.

Shortly, Joshua heard a rumor (v. 16) that the Gibeonites were, in fact, only their neighbors and had actually deceived them. Whereupon, he made a short journey and learned the truth (v. 17). Matters were worse than they appeared. Not only were the Gibeonites their neighbors, but they were just one of four cities in the Hivite kingdom which was in collusion with them. How could Joshua have made such a mistake? There is a very fine line between acting upon circumstances as they are, and circumstances as they only appear to be. But it is an extremely important line, and one that he unwittingly crossed.

He had done what God had told him to do in allowing inhabitants of the wilderness to serve them, but it was a decision made only on partial truth. God's directions, therefore, were misapplied, and the results were devastating. Joshua did what God had told him to do under the circumstances, but the circumstances were not what they appeared to be; therefore, Joshua was wrong.

The only thing he could do then was to settle for second best and make a pact with these people. Indeed, God gave them a measure of victory, humiliating the Gibeonites into becoming their servants, cutting wood for the continual burnt offering and bearing water for the cleansing rites in the place of worship. It was all right, but it was not the best. The consequences of a sin which is the result of deception are not as severe as for a sin which is the result of blatant willfulness. But there are consequences to be paid, nonetheless. These people remained forever a consistent agitation to the children of God. They should have been destroyed, but Satan's deception had now made that impossible.

Two wrongs don't make a right. They had sworn in the name

of Jehovah to live in league with the Gibeonites, and once the promise had been made, the treaty could not be broken. They had to live with consequences of the devil's successful attempt to deceive them because they had failed to follow the spiritual direction God had made available to them. Though they were less severe than the consequences of rebellion, they were devastating, nonetheless. The devil will take what he can get. The resolution of the issue, to live as their servants, though a perpetual thorn in Israel's side, appears to be all the Gibeonites were looking for in the first place (vv. 9,11). They were satisfied but Israel was not. Nothing less than perfection would do as the standard for Joshua and the people of God. But Lucifer will settle for a toehold. "We are better to serve Israel and live than fight Israel and die," they reasoned! When Jesus cast several demons out of the demoniac of Gadara, they pleaded to be sent into the swine to live, rather than cast into the lake of fire before their time.

Oh, the deception of Satan. What he cannot do in a frontal attack, he will do from within. And he does it so often and so adroitly in the lives of well-meaning people who misinterpret and misapply the Word of God. The temptation of Satan to Christ on the "pinnacle of the temple" was "Cast thyself down from hence . . . his angels . . . shall, bear thee up, lest at any time thou dash thy foot against a stone." That was, indeed, truth from Scripture, but it was truth misapplied. Our Lord's response was to use the Scripture correctly and he replied, "It is said, Thou shalt not tempt the Lord thy God" (Luke 4:9-12).

Our Lord has given us far too many tools with which to know his Word properly and do his will for us ever to succumb to Lucifer's deception. Let us be "instant in season, out of season" (2 Tim. 4:2), and diligent in "rightly dividing the word" (v. 15).

9
No Compromise

Joshua 10:1-43

At Jericho we learned the importance of trust and obedience in spite of all earthly appearance and human substance. At Ai our Lord spoke clearly to us about the influence of evil on the life of the entire believing family and of the necessity of strict separation from evil. The league with the wily Gibeonites in chapter 9 has impressed upon us (1) the skill of the enemy in twisting the Word of God to deceive us and (2) the futility of human reason.

Let it never be forgotten that there was no excuse for Joshua's failure in handling Gibeon. His conscience, his Lord, and the high priest were all at his disposal, but were neglected. Here, as other places, Joshua, as the perfect type of Christ, obviously breaks down. At any rate, Joshua had learned his lesson well. Toward the end of this chapter we find him making giant strides in the normal life-style of the victorious believer.

Each of the battles fought by the Israelites pictures a distinct spiritual truth that must be learned by the victorious Christian warrior. In chapter 10 the lesson is that every remnant of evil must go to the minutest detail if absolute victory is to be experienced. The enemy must be rooted out completely. Joshua courageously gave chase to all the struggling warriors in the army of the wicked and would not be thwarted in his goal for total victory. The application is obviously for the Christian, and it is a lesson of vast importance.

Chapter 10 continues sequentially the story of the abortive union of Israel with the pagan Gibeonites. The union never should have occurred in the first place, but Joshua had given his word to protect Gibeon, and protect it he did. Because of his sincerity, sorrow, repentance, and faith, this bad experience turned out for the good, though not for the best. The league with Gibeon was not the perfect will of God, and Israel had to settle for second best.

In the first six verses of the chapter, a second league of kings again formed a confederation to fight against Israel. The confederation listed in the first two verses of the previous chapter was approximately forty miles away, and this new one was much closer. Surely they had heard of the plan of their northern neighbors to attempt to stop Israel by taking league with their fellows, and planned to do the same. Being closer to Israel, their need was at once imminent and perilous, and they were filled with great fear.

The united army was formed at the bidding of King Adonizedec, and plans were made to carry the battle to Joshua and his troops. Joshua would not be caught off guard again. Already he was acting upon a well-thought-out plan and had pressed westward toward the heart of Jericho, dividing the people to the north and south, defeating both Jericho and Ai in the central campaign. This second effort—the southern campaign—would find Israel in headlong confrontation with Adonizedec and his cohorts. The third campaign—the northern campaign—would be fought by the waters of Merom. This effort is recorded in chapter 11 and entails little more than a mopping-up effort of a land long since delivered by God into the hand of the Israelites.

Adonizedec was king of Jerusalem and may well be a type of the devil. As a "Melchizedek" type of Christ means "king of righteousness," Adonizedec means "lord of righteousness." We are thereby immediately confronted with a Christ-type religious leader. He was at once an unbelieving king who is both anti-Christ and anti-God. In this he perfectly pictures Satan, who is the author of all counterfeit religion and who will even occupy the throne of Jerusalem, one day to be occupied by none other than King Jesus himself (Luke 1:32).

Adonizedec panicked upon hearing what Joshua had done to Ai and Jericho. Note that this Satan type only heard. Often we are asked if Satan knows our thoughts, and the answer is a resounding no. He is smart and observant. He knows much, says much, and hears much. He knows the Word of God and knows how to twist it. But he doesn't know everything, and he doesn't know what's in our thoughts. Having heard that this powerful foe was now in league with the Gibeonites, he feared greatly.

It is important for the believer to remember that positionally Satan is a defeated foe and has every reason to fear the people of God. He was banished from heaven, defeated at Calvary, and will be cast into the lake of fire. He knows his days are numbered and that he can go no farther than God allows. While we must give him his due, let it be remembered that complete victory by the power of the blood, by the indwelling Christ, and by the Word of God is available to even the weakest of God's children. "Greater is he that is in you, than he that is in the world" (1 John 4:4).

What a pity that the church often trembles before the onslaughts of an evil world and only responds to its threats.

The militant body of Christ should be shaping the world, not reacting to it.

Specifically, his fear of Israel's league with the city of Gibeon was because it was a great, large, and royal city, and as the capital, well-fortified, a city stronger even than powerful Ai, and whose men were well-known for their force and strength (v. 2). We are intrigued with Adonizedec's preoccupation with attacking Gibeon simply because they were now in league with Israel. Perhaps they acted out of frustration or fear.

Gibeon, a greater force with which to be reckoned than even Jericho or Ai, was enough to make Adonizedec tremble. If Israel could defeat those two cities, what could they now do, joining forces with an even greater ally? But in the mind of the kings of the mountains (v. 6) something had to be done. It is quite possible that the spiritual analogy of this attack may best be understood in terms of Gibeon as a former ally which the wicked kings could not easily let go. Once an unbeliever has deserted the ranks of the evil one to give allegiance to King Jesus, he becomes twofold the object of hell's fury and Satan's open attack. The enemy does not easily let go his own.

Upon learning of the imminent attack of the kings (v. 6), the men of Gibeon immediately cried to Joshua for help. It is of interest that they knew precisely where to find the Israelites. Joshua and the people of God would be camped at Gilgal. Following every defeat and every victory, they returned to the place where God initially met them in the Promised Land. The simplest basics of the Christian faith indicate: we need to meet God consistently. Here, particularly after victory, the threat of pride could enter. The need to retreat into the presence of God may be far greater following victory than defeat. They knew precisely that was the place to find Joshua. The unbelieving world should not look for the believer in the bars and clubs, but in the house of God.

The response of Joshua was immediate (v. 7). Our heavenly Joshua is always swift to act. Only a prayer away awaits all of the power of the universe to those who need and trust the Lord. The promise of our Lord to give victory to Joshua in spite of the mistaken allegiance with Gibeon (v. 8) occasions great encouragement in the heart of the penitent. Joshua should never have been in this position in the first place, but he was, and he had learned, and he was sorry.

Again comes the good news of the second chance, "Fear them not: for I have delivered them into thine hand" (v. 8). In the First World War, for instance, Japan was our ally. In the Second, Japan was our bitter enemy. On the constant changing horizon of world events, yesterday's enemy is today's friend, and yesterday's friend, today's enemy. One must wonder how world leaders, as did Joshua, continue to go from mistake to mistake, failing to call upon Him upon whose shoulders are the governments of the world.

But take heart. As with Joshua, God is ready to forgive and to offer another opportunity. Joshua's reply to their plea was swift and immediate. Riding all night, the soldiers of Israel found an easy victory over the opposing armies, for the Lord had weakened their spirits ("discomfited them," v. 10) before Israel arrived.

The victory at Gibeon was called "a great slaughter," but that is not complete. The key to the chapter is the word *chased* in verse 10. Many enemy stragglers ran away and had to be pursued, as described in the remainder of the chapter. Joshua had learned his lesson well, and this time none of the enemy remnant would escape. As they were fleeing (v. 11), God miraculously came to Israel's aid with a giant hailstorm.

I have said previously that all of the universe is in opposition to the man who sets himself against God. Here, conversely, our Lord arranged even the natural forces of heaven to harmonize with the efforts of those completely committed to doing his will. The enemy fled before Israel, and the Israelites gave chase. When we are sincerely committed to the pursuit of righteousness, the wicked one flees and the Lord comes to our aid. "Resist the devil and, he will flee from you" (Jas. 4:7).

As the day wore on, the Lord who had fought for Israel with hailstones before in Egypt was still not through fighting for his own. So completely committed was Joshua to total victory that he pursued the enemy until sunset and then commanded the sun and moon to stand still that the job might be completed (v. 12). While there are those who make pitiful attempts to disdain this mighty miracle, let it be simply stated that the God who created the sun and the moon and all that is, is more than pleased to control even the elements to allow total success when his children serve him.

At the beginning of verse 12 Joshua spoke to the Lord—at the end of the verse he spoke to the sun—and that in full view of the people. No man would dare speak *for* the Lord who had not first spoken *to* the Lord. The writer of Joshua makes two important comments about this miracle (vv. 13-15).

First, it is recorded in the book of Jasher, probably a type of poetic record of Israel's military campaigns and, second, it was perhaps the greatest answer to prayer in the history of the world. The author was so impressed, as are we, that he added the inspired footnote that never did the Lord harken to the voice of a man in such a way as when the Lord gave Israel victory by the staying of the sun and moon. This is found in Joshua 10:12-14.

But the battle was not over, and Joshua must have further directions. In spite of earthly and heavenly effort, fragmented, but powerful, forces yet eluded Israel's onslaught. Joshua would have none of it. Partial victory was no victory at all, and it was back to Gilgal to wait before God. At the height of the battle (v. 16), the five kings fled for their lives, and hid in a cave at Makkedah. How unlike our Commander in Chief who said, "I will never leave you nor forsake you," and "Lo, I am with you alway, even unto the end of the world" (Matt. 28:20).

But Joshua would deal with the kings at another time. A stone was rolled over the mouth of the cave (v. 18), and they were secured for the present. The issue was the business at hand, and there were yet remnants of the enemy to be hunted down and destroyed.

Here is a mighty picture of the millennium. We have seen at the outset of the chapter that Adonizedec was an anti-type of Christ, and pretender to his throne. During the millennium, Satan will be bound for a thousand years while the Lord brings peace on earth. At the end of that time he will be loosed a little season, judged, and banished forever to the lake of fire. This same release for judgment and execution awaited the enemy kings (vv. 23,26).

The immediate issue is the constant pursuit of the last remnant of the enemy. "Pursue after your enemies, and smite the hindmost of them; suffer them not to enter into their cities" was the command of Joshua (v. 19). "Do not stop now. Victory is at hand, and the Lord has promised it to you." The last hiding place would be back in their cities and they must not be allowed to escape there (v. 19). That, however, is precisely what happened (v. 20). And even there they would be pursued and utterly destroyed (v. 28).

The mature believer must deal with the tiniest fragments of sin to the last degree if complete victory is to be assured. Every former physical relationship and reminder of forsaken evil must be ferreted out, confessed, and forsaken. It is often true that even the memory of such sin can be the last holdout of the enemy. But even this is not beyond the reach of the blood of Christ. The subconscious mind, as well as the conscious, may be brought to the cleansing light of Calvary where, by faith, he is well able to cleanse to the uttermost, even the memory of evil buried deep in the subconscious mind.

The king of Jerusalem and his counterparts must not be allowed to remain alive in the cave. Imprisonment was not sufficient. They must be slaughtered. As Satan will be released for a little season in the end and then cast into eternal judgment, so the remnant of all sin must be brought to light, judged, and annihilated.

Joshua, in verse 24, with a flair for the dramatic, commanded his captains to place their feet on the necks of the enemy kings as a visual testimony that God had given victory over all their enemies (v. 25). The picture of Israel's feet on enemy necks is one fraught with spiritual truth. Feet in the Bible were often picture authority. In the ancient world monarchs were always exalted on thrones. Kneeling before them in submission, a subject would look up and see the feet of the emperor. The exalted position of feet always spoke of the authority of the ruler. The neck has a similar significance. Knowledge, emotion, and will reside in the head, but express themselves in the body. The neck, then, is the supply line from the source to the action. The picture of Israel's feet upon enemy necks signifies the believer's authority over evil at its very source. Destroy the neck and the body is dead. Cut off the lifeline and the enemy is defeated.

In Christ, authority, power, and victory are complete, even to the source and lifeline of evil. We must go to the source; we must ferret out the roots and destroy to the uttermost the presence of evil and its influence by the authority that is ours in the Word of God and Christ's own victory.

Here, as in chapter 9, the enemy kings were hanged on trees in public ridicule as our Lord made open display of the futility of satanic power under the authority and control of his lordship. Victory over Satan is possible. But only if it is complete and uncompromising, Satan and nothing that he is or has must remain in the believer's life.

The remainder of the chapter, in what has come to be known as the southern campaign (v. 40), is important because of what it does not say. Joshua had learned his lesson well. The miraculous had become commonplace and he walked in such fellowship with God that each ensuing battle and its immediate victory is described in the most common terms. Without comment, and in stride, the writer records simply that Joshua utterly defeated Makkedah, Libnah, Lachish, Gezer, Eglon, Hebron, and Debir. Nothing spectacular, nothing miraculous— just victory after victory.

This is the "normal Christian life," as Watchman Nee described it. It is the way of life for the believer and it is one of consistent victory and Christian normality. But it is only possible once the lessons of earlier campaigns have been learned, and learned well: God must be obeyed at all costs. Sin in the camp must never be tolerated; Satan must not deceive us with the Word; and the enemy must be pursued to the last detail and utterly annihilated.

One might well imagine that a man now walking in such daily victory could easily be filled with pride and made to stumble. But such was not the case with Joshua. The reason for his unparalleled success is found in verse 43, and is at once a fitting commentary and conclusion to Joshua's victory.

"And Joshua returned, and all Israel with him, unto the camp to Gilgal."

10
Victory Is Costly

Joshua 11:1 to 12:1

Joshua 11:2 relates that this final confederation of enemy kings dwelt on the north side of the mountains. We have examined the central campaign of approximately two weeks, the southern campaign of about a year, and come now to the final effort, the battle of the northern campaign, lasting five or six years. Remembering that Joshua was to Israel what Jesus is to the believer, we are not surprised to see a final all-out effort by the forces of evil against the children of Israel.

It was the enemy king who took the initiative, who gathered his forces, and made a final effort against the people of God. At the forefront of the battle, Joshua confronted Jabin, king of Hazor and captain of the enemy hosts, in a final showdown for the land of Canaan. It is Satan's ultimate effort against King Jesus and a perfect picture of the battle that was fought at the cross where Satan made his last-ditch stand to keep hold on the kingdom of the human heart. There he was soundly defeated once for all by him who is the "Captain of their salvation" (Heb. 3:10), none other than Christ himself.

Following there were only mopping-up exercises. Herein the land would be secured, and that which had been won positionally would now be claimed experientially. Let us look for a moment at the character of the enemy, King Jabin.

We are at once impressed that the meaning of his name allows a dead giveaway as to the true character of his nature. The word *Jabin* means "the wise" or "the intelligent."

Jabin's counterpart in the south was named Adonizedec. In control of both the north and south, they joined together to form a perfect picture of him who walks "to and fro in the earth, and from walking up and down in it" (Job 1:7; 2:2), totally in control of the kingdom of the heart. In control, that is, until confronted by our heavenly Joshua. As Adonizedec, lord of righteousness, was a false religious personage, so Jabin, the wise, completes the picture of the wicked one. It was Satan's pseudo wisdom and infatuation with his own beauty that led him to rebel against the Father. He appealed to Eve in the Garden that the fruit was something "to make one wise." "For the Jews require a sign, and the Greeks seek after wisdom" (1 Cor. 1:22). And it is the way of God still.

> For it is written, I will destroy the wisdom of the wise, and will bring to nothing the understanding of the prudent. Where is the wise? where is the scribe? where is the disputer of this world? hath not God made foolish the wisdom of this world? For after that in the wisdom of God the world by wisdom knew not God, it pleased God by the foolishness of preaching to save them that believe. For the Jews require a sign, and the Greeks seek after wisdom: But we preach Christ crucified, unto the Jews a stumbling-block, and unto the Greeks foolishness; But unto them which are called, both Jews and Greeks, Christ the power of God, and the wisdom of God. Because the foolishness of God is wiser than men; and the weakness of God is stronger than men. For ye see your calling, brethren, how that not many wise men after the flesh, not many mighty, not many noble, are called: But God hath chosen the foolish things of the world to confound the wise; and God hath chosen the weak things of the world to confound the things

> which are mighty; And base things of the world, and things which are despised, hath God chosen, yea, and things which are not, to bring to nought things that are: That no flesh should glory in his presence (1 Cor. 1:19-29).

Jabin's actions complete the picture of Lucifer in his control over an innumerable army (v. 4). The statement that the number of soldiers was as large as the sands of the seashore is, of course, hyperbole. It was common for the ancients to use this device for purposes of emphasis. Jeremiah said, "Their widows are increased to me above the sands of the sea" (15:8), and Nahum, "[Nineveh hath more merchants than] the stars of heaven" (3:16). But regardless of the number, and Josepheus estimated it between 300,000 to 400,000, it was (1) convened by Jabin; (2) extremely large in scope; (3) under specific direction and appointment of Jabin (they met together, v. 5a); and (4) joined in a common cause to "fight against Israel" (v. 5b).

Carrying the analogy still further, whence came the army of demonic evil spirits over which Satan reigns in this world. Isaiah tells us that he who rebelled against the authority of God would be "brought down to hell, to the sides of the pit" (14:15). Lucifer, then, is pictured as having been cast down here from heaven above. Jesus carried out that line of logic when he, too, described Satan's fall. "And the seventy returned again with joy, saying, Lord, even the devils are subject unto us through thy name. And he said unto them, I beheld Satan as lightning fall from heaven" (Luke 10:17-18).

In context, our Lord is referring to his authority over all demonic forces, which authority he has given those who minister in his name.

The Revelation writer carries the theme still further:

> And there appeared another wonder in heaven; and behold a great red dragon, having seven heads and ten horns, and seven crowns upon his

heads. And his tail drew the third part of the stars of heaven, and did cast them to the earth: and the dragon stood before the woman which was ready to be delivered, for to devour her child as soon as it was born. And she brought forth a man child, who was to rule all nations with a rod of iron: and her child was caught up unto God, and to his throne. And the woman fled into the wilderness, where she hath a place prepared of God, that they should feed her there a thousand two hundred and threescore days. And there was war in heaven: Michael and his angels fought against the dragon; and the dragon fought and his angels, And prevailed not; neither was their place found any more in heaven. And the great dragon was cast out, that old serpent, called the Devil, and Satan, which deceiveth the whole world: he was cast out into the earth, and his angels were cast out with him (Rev. 12:3-9).

It appears from Scripture that before life was created on earth the Father, Son, and Holy Spirit presided over an angelic society in heaven directed by three archangels—Michael, Lucifer, and Gabriel. When Lucifer's heart was filled with pride, he declared war on God and was joined by one third of the stars (angels) who sided with him. The archangel, Michael, fought against Lucifer and the rebellious angels and defeated them. When the dragon was banished and fell to earth, the rebellious angels followed him. It is obvious to me that the vast network of evil spirits or demonic forces over which Lucifer presides in this world are, in fact, those fallen angels.

No sooner was the challenge laid down before Joshua than it was immediately picked up. Our Lord will fight the battle and deliver them into Israel's hands "to-morrow about this time" (v. 6). You will notice also in the sixth verse that God said he would deliver them. In verse 7, Joshua came to fight the war, and in verse 8 the Lord delivered them. It is imperative to understand that the victory was the Lord's, but men did the fighting. So it is in the spiritual battle. It is "not by might, nor by power, but by my spirit, saith the Lord" (Zech. 4:16), that the battle is won. But it is ours to stand daily with the Word of God and the shield of faith, allowing the Lord to be victorious in battle through our lives.

Joshua had learned well the lesson at Ai. No residue of evil would be allowed here. The victory must be as complete as it was great. "They smote them, until they left none remaining" (v. 8). Even the chariots were destroyed and the horses hocked (v. 9). This means that the "hamstrings" in back of the horse's rear legs were severed. The animal could never again be ridden as an instrument of war against Israel, but the offspring it would produce would be a healthy instrument in the hands of the people of God. How superior is our Lord to the evil one. How beautifully he outcrafts the deceiver in turning evil to good. Let it be well remembered in the defeat of the enemy army under Jabin that unity is not always strength. Far more is it to be desired that we bind ourselves together in truth, rather than simply by great numbers.

Nor does the visible always correspond with the actual. This was the first time that Israel ever confronted an army equal to or numbering more than themselves. But to the "Captain of the Lord's hosts," the General of our "invisible army," the size of the opposition made no difference. He who is able to "save them the uttermost" (Heb. 7:25) is able to "succour them that are tempted" (Heb. 2:18).

We are impressed with the swiftness of Joshua's immediate response and the obvious courage of his heart. Although the Psalms had not been written, surely appropriate thoughts similar to Psalm 91:1-7 must have been racing through his mind.

He that dwelleth in the secret place of the most High shall abide under the shadow of the Almighty. I will say of the Lord, He is my refuge and my fortress: my God; in him will I trust. Surely he shall deliver thee from the snare of the fowler, and from the noisome pestilence. He shall cover thee with his feathers, and under his wings shalt thou

> trust: his truth shall be thy shield and buckler. Thou shalt not be afraid for the terror by night; nor for the arrow that flieth by day; Nor for the pestilence that walketh in darkness; nor for the destruction that wasteth at noonday. A thousand shall fall at thy side, and ten thousand at thy right hand; but it shall not come nigh thee.

Not only was the army soundly defeated, but Jabin's throne city of Hazor was burned with fire (v. 11). Even so, will Satan be cast into the lake of fire forever at the end of time. "And the devil that deceived them was cast into the lake of fire and brimstone, where the beast and the false prophet are, and shall be tormented day and night for ever and ever" (Rev. 20:10).

Verse 18 states simply that the war lasted a long time. We believe from Caleb's testimony in chapter 14 that it took about five years. Every enemy was utterly destroyed as the Lord did "harden their hearts" (v. 20) to advance into the trap of Israel's God. When a people are going with God, all of the forces of nature and human personality are under the control of their God to arrange for victory in their hearts.

Verses 21 and 22 obviously refer to a very special, isolated campaign against the Anakims, which Joshua saved until last. And who were those Anakims, and why are they special? When Joshua and Caleb returned from Canaan forty-five years before, they reported that the portion of the land they had seen was filled with great "giants—the sons of Anak" (Num. 13:33). The Anakims were the giant people Joshua himself had seen, and he was not at all anxious to go up against them. Each of us has that giant in his life that we most fear. Though we save it until last, even it must be brought under the annihilation of Joshua's sword. Christ must slay every giant of the human heart.

The victory was great, but unfortunately, it was not complete. None of the Anakims were left except in Gaza, Gath, and Ashdod (v. 22). Unfortunately, it was the remnant of that very people which was allowed to escape to Gath that would ultimately produce Goliath of the Philistines who would one day threaten their descendants.

> And there went out a champion out of the camp of the Philistines, named Goliath, of Gath, whose height was six cubits and a span. And he had an helmet of brass upon his head, and he was armed with a coat of mail; and the weight of the coat was five thousand shekels of brass. And he had greaves of brass upon his legs, and a target of brass between his shoulders. And the staff of his spear was like a weaver's beam; and his spear's head weighed six hundred shekels of iron: and one bearing a shield went before him. And he stood and cried unto the armies of Israel, and said unto them, Why are ye come out to set your battle in array? am not I a Philistine, and ye servants to Saul? choose you a man for you, and let him come down to me. If he be able to fight with me, and to kill me, then will we be your servants: but if I prevail against him, and kill him, then shall ye be our servants, and serve us. And the Philistine said, I defy the armies of Israel this day; give me a man, that we may fight together. When Saul and all Israel heard those words of the Philistine, they were dismayed, and greatly afraid (1 Sam. 17:4-11).

As surely as we allow the giants in our lives to escape the annihilating sword of the Savior, they will come back to haunt us in our lives and in the lives of our children. "For I the Lord thy God am a jealous God, visiting the iniquity of the fathers upon the children unto the third and fourth generation of them that hate me" (Ex. 20:5*b*).

Before we conclude our study with the last verse of chapter 11, let us note that the twelfth chapter is a summary of all the kings destroyed and battles won in the three campaigns for Canaan. These are probably recorded again in the book of Jasher, some type of chronicle of Israel's military campaigns forever lost. It is of interest to note that thirty-one kings had been vanquished. Before Roman and Arabic numerals were used, an intricate system of numbering called gematria was employed to designate numbers by letters of the alphabet. In gematria, 31 was the number for *el,* the Hebrew name for God. The picture is a beautiful one. Our God is the perfect match for all of the enemies of the human heart. Thirty-one battles, and God is adequate. Thirty-one thousand battles, and he is adequate still. "Greater is he that is in you, than he that is in the world" (1 John 4:4). "If God be for us, who can be against us?" (Rom. 8:31).

At the conclusion of the eleventh chapter, the land was secured and rested from war. Much territory yet remained to be claimed by each tribe, but the major battles were over, the enemy was beaten, and Canaan was under the control of Israel. The land resting from war is a perfect picture of our High Priest, the heavenly Joshua, seated at the right hand of the Father, appropriating his blood, providing experientially the daily victory that he has secured positionally at the cross.

Our Lord's last words at Calvary were, "It is finished" (John 19:30). That was not a cry of futility or of failure, but the cry of victory. He did not say, "*I* am finished." At Calvary, Satan had mustered all of his forces against Christ who had defeated "him that had the power of death, that is, the devil" (Heb. 2:14).

And the land rested from war and Joshua rested from conflict. It was not a rest of exhaustion, but of composure and complete victory. The heart that is safely trusting in Christ need not live in frustration and spiritual fatigue from the battle. For if such be the case, we only struggle in the flesh. I am reminded of Paul's plaintive plea, "Oh, wretched man that I am! who shall deliver me from the body of this death?" (Rom. 7:24), can only be answered, "Thanks be to God, which giveth us the victory through our Lord Jesus Christ" (1 Cor. 15:57).

11
Joshua Was Old . . .
but Bold

Joshua 13:1-8,14,22; 14:6-13; 15:16-19; 16:1

The thirteenth chapter marks an important division in the Book of Joshua. The land had been secured at the hand of Joshua. God had given the victory through the obedience and faith of his faithful servant and his followers, "and yet there remaineth very much land to be possessed" (v. 1). The secured victory would have to be appropriated and used by the tribes. A part of Joshua's reward was rest from battle. Yet, his greatest accomplishment lay before him. What good is victory secured without appropriation? Of what profit was conquered Canaan without appropriation? The title deed was in their hands, and now it was time to move in and inhabit the new property.

This awesome responsibility was entrusted to the faithful Joshua. He who had ordered the sun and moon to stand still in the presence of Israel would not be challenged by the tribes. The minister, like the lawyer and the doctor but unlike the athlete, may be at his prime during the older years. A new job for Joshua was the order of the day. Though "old and stricken in years," there was no need for him to be set on the shelf. The

new responsibility, though less strenuous, was just as important as the former, and one he was prepared to handle. It is a
grave error when the young do not look to the aged for the
benefit of wisdom that only age can bring.

The land now secured must now become the land possessed.
It would be apropos to say that if Texas were under the control
of an invading army and only Houston, San Antonio, Dallas,
and Fort Worth were secured, fierce opposition could be
expected in the outlying regions. What has been won must now
be grasped. The gift of victory that faith provided must now be
appropriated by the individual tribes. John 3:16 reminds us that
God gave his Son. And Romans 6:23 adds that salvation is the
"gift of God." Yet the clear teaching of Scripture is "fight the
good fight of faith, lay hold on eternal life" (1 Tim. 6:12).

The cooperation between a victory secured by faith, but
achieved by human effort, may be seen in the maturation of a
tree to fruit-bearing. Though only God can make a tree and
give it the life to grow and bear fruit, one must plant the tree
and cultivate it. It is by cooperating with God in pruning and
spraying the sapling that it might come to productivity.

To continue this thought, let us omit, for the time being, our
study of verses 2 through 5 and resume the story in verse 6. At
the conclusion of God's description of the land yet to be
possessed, he states, "them will I drive out . . . only divide
thou it by lot unto the Israelites for an inheritance." God had
promised to drive out their enemies only on the condition that
they proceed with dividing up the land and possessing it. It
was, "I will if you will." One may safely assume that if they
did not do their part to possess the land, God would not fulfill
the contingent promise to drive out the remaining forces
inhabiting the extremities of Canaan.

The analogy is carried further in the instruction of the sixth
verse to divide up the land "by lot." The practice of making

decisions within the sovereignty of God by drawing lots was long since established with the command to the high priest to select the black or white stone, the Urim and Thummim, from his breastplate in deciding issues of national importance. It was followed in New Testament days when the disciples chose Matthias by lot to be the twelfth disciple when Judas fell.

A careful study of Scripture, however, will remind us that this is the second and seeming different direction give to Israel to determine the division of the land.

> And the Lord spake unto Moses, saying, Unto these the land shall be divided for an inheritance according to the number of names. To many thou shalt give the more inheritance, and to few thou shalt give the less inheritance: to every one shall his inheritance be given according to those that were numbered of him. Notwithstanding the land shall be divided by lot: according to the names of the tribes of their fathers they shall inherit. According to the lot shall the possession thereof be divided between many and few (Num. 26:52-56).

The division of Canaan, then, was to be made on the basis of size, as well as drawing. On the one hand it was clearly stated that the large tribes were to have larger pieces of land, and the small tribes, smaller sections. However, the choice was to be made by drawing names from a common bowl. How may these two concepts be harmonized? By the human response that acts in obedience and faith to a sovereign God. A similar procedure was followed in the Book of Acts (6) when lots were cast to select Matthias as an apostle. Again the principle of human action within the scope of divine power was established. God may be trusted to guide perfectly the affairs of men who respond to him with absolute obedience.

Returning again for a look at verses 2-6, we discover the precise description of the unpossessed land given by the Lord. He who points out the remote areas yet to be conquered will be faithful to describe them specifically. It is never necessary for us to wander in the dark regarding those unconquered territories of our hearts. If we are sincere in our desire to discern the giants that remain to be slain within us, God will be faithful to point them out.

Verses 7-12 describe the division of the two and one-half tribes, the Reubenites, the Gadites, and the half tribe of Manasseh that chose to remain on the other side of Jordan. It appears from the text that no choice was given them and no drawing held in their behalf. They had chosen to settle for second best and would take what they got. It is a pity that people do the same today. Verse 13 records their failure to completely expel the remaining portions of two enemies that lingered for years. Those extremities of the heart not conquered by Christ will one day come to haunt us.

In the division of the land we are reminded in verse 14, and again in verse 33, that no inheritance was given to the Levites. The Levitical priesthood established for the tribe of Levi provided that they owned no physical bit of the property, but were suported by the entire congregation. Their inheritance is "the sacrifices of the Lord God of Israel made by fire" ((v. 14). Their reward, far greater than any piece of land, was the joy of the service of the Lord. Supported by the people they served, for "they which preach the gospel should live of the gospel" (1 Cor. 10:14), their ministry was their reward. The apostle Paul said of those whom he had won to Christ, "[You are] our joy, . . . or crown of rejoicing" (1 Thess. 2:19).

The division of the land on the other side of Jordan to the two and one-half tribes who chose to remain are as follows: The land for the Reubenites (vv. 15-23); the land for the Gadites (vv. 24-28); the land for the half tribe of Manasseh (29-31).

There is a brief, but important, side thought to the story of the possession of the land in verse 22. When entering the land of Midian (v. 21), the children of Israel found the false prophet Balaam and slew him (v. 22). Years before, Balaam had been hired by Balak, king of the Midianites, to put an evil curse on Israel. Powerless to do so he offered Balak a superior plan by which to destroy the Israelites: Let the daughters of the Midianites intermarry with the sons of Israel and corrupt them with Midianite idolatry. The results were as devastating as they were swift. Balaam was rewarded and settled down to live among the Midianites. Invading the land of Midian, the tribe of Reuben found Balaam and killed him. He who had chosen to live with the people of death had, at the last, died with them, as well.

Chapter 14 begins with the division of the land on the Canaan side of Jordan among the nine and one-half remaining tribes. The half tribe of Manasseh grew again to a full tenth tribe; the Levites living among all the people were the eleventh tribe; and Ephraim, the son of Joseph, was the twelfth tribe. Joseph, the father of twin sons, Manasseh and Ephraim, was rewarded for his faithfulness in Egypt by having his sons as the heads of tribes. Here he was a beautiful picture of the Savior who preserved the life of his brethren down in Egypt, bestowed upon them considerable gifts, and is honored among his sons. We who love Jesus who has saved us, should also honor him, since we are his family.

The first verse of chapter 14 states that the actual division of the land was under the supervision of Joshua, Eleazar, the high priest, and the heads of the tribes. These three form a picture of the Trinity presiding over the affairs of the believer in heaven. The heart of the fourteenth chapter is the marvelous story of the faith of the aged Caleb. Forty-five years before, upon their return from surveying the land of Israel, it was Caleb who spoke up and urged Moses and the Israelites to trust

God and proceed. "And Caleb stilled the people before Moses, and said, Let us go up at once, and possess it; for we are well able to overcome it" (Num. 13:30). Thereupon, God promised that Caleb would be given the precise land upon which he had stood when the children of Israel possessed the land forty-five years later.

> Surely they shall not see the land which I sware unto their fathers, neither shall any of them that provoked me see it: But my servant Caleb, because he had another spirit with him, and hath followed me fully, him will I bring into the land whereinto he went; and his seed shall possess it. (Now the Amalekites and the Canaanites dwelt in the valley.) To-morrow, turn you, and get you into the wilderness by the way of the Red sea (Num. 14:23-25).

The land, as may be seen from verse 25 above and from previous studies, was the land of the Amalekites wherein were the Anakims, the strain of great giants. For years the promise had burned in Caleb's heart (Josh. 14:6).

As a member of the tribe of Judah, whose lot was to be drawn first, Caleb knew that if Judah did not draw the name of the area with his (Caleb's) mountain on it, the promise of God could not be fulfilled. It was now time for Caleb to speak. Courageously he reminded Joshua of God's promise in verse 9: "And Moses sware on that day, saying, Surely the land whereon thy feet have trodden shall be thine inheritance, and thy children's for ever, because thou hast wholly followed the Lord my God," and boldly claimed what was his: "Now therefore give me this mountain, whereof the Lord spake in that day; for thou heardest in that day how the Anakims were there, and that the cities were great and fenced: if so be the Lord will be with me, then I shall be able to drive them out, as the Lord said" (Josh. 14:12). That kind of praying can get nothing except a swift and affirmative response from the Lord. Joshua answered positively and granted the request (v. 13).

Why was Caleb so eager to have that particular mountain? The answer is simple. For forty-five years he had chafed under the blighting accusation of Israel that Jehovah God was incapable of handling the problem of the giants. God could slay the giants. God could do anything, and Caleb wanted the chance to prove it once and for all. The honor of God must be vindicated.

"Don't think that just because I am eighty-five years old I cannot handle the problem of the giants," Caleb said, "for I am as strong this day as I ever was" (see vv. 10-11). How could Caleb be so bold? Because his unabating strength came from an abiding faith in God. Caleb had another spirit within him and followed the Lord freely (Num. 14:24). It was the joint testimony of both Joshua and Caleb that the people of the land were not to be feared, for "the Lord is with us" (14:9).

The fifteenth chapter begins with the first lot drawn for the lands of Canaan. It was, of course, the tribe of Judah. The sixteenth chapter begins with the second drawing in Canaan for the children of Joseph—Ephraim and Manasseh. The order of procedure among the tribes was always Judah first, and the sons of Joseph second. Though Reuben was the firstborn, he had defiled his father's bed and his birthright was given to Joseph. Judah prevailed above his brethren and became the chief ruler, but Israel's birthright was Joseph's.

Accordingly, the division of the land was in three successive stages: First, the settlement of Judah in the strongholds in the south (ch. 15); second, the settlement of Joseph's sons, Ephraim and Manasseh, in the center of the country (ch. 16); and third, the settlement of the remaining tribes to fill in the gaps between Judah and Joseph and was upon the outskirts of their territory so as to be under the shelter of their protecting wings.

Let us go back for a moment to the drawing for Judah (15:1), and recall that Joshua had promised Caleb a specific area as a part of the tribe of Judah. Yet, the drawing of the lot for Judah continued. How could Joshua have done such a thing? What if a lot was drawn that did not include the land promised to Caleb, the Judahite? Undoubtedly, Joshua's faith in God to fulfill his promise was so strong that he proceeded unhesitatingly.

Again the picture of human response working within the framework of divine sovereignty may be seen. Joshua will act in faith, and God will give the victory. Joshua had learned that lesson far too well to hesitate. We may take great courage in knowing that our Lord will arrange the affairs of an entire nation to fulfill his promise to one man who has the courage to boldly say, "Give me this mountain!"

Within the account of the description of the land selected for the tribe of Judah, there is a further story of the boldness of a faith that would not be denied (15:16-19). Caleb had destroyed all of the giants of his inheritance, including the three sons of Anak, the chief, after whom the entire race was named. Anak himself obviously dwelt in the chief city of Kirjathsepher.

Caleb was old and ready for help. "He that smiteth Kirjathsepher, . . . to him will I give Achsah my daughter, to wife" (v. 16). Othniel obviously loved Achsah and claimed the offer, taking the city and winning the prize of Caleb's daughter. As his future son-in-law had been inspired by Caleb's abounding faith to seize the prize offered him, just so was Achsah moved to ask boldly what she desired. The land wherein she would dwell with Othniel was a "south land" (barren and with little water—v. 19). "Give me a blessing," she cried. "What wouldst thou?" (v. 18). "Give me also springs of water," and he gave her "the upper and the nether springs" (v. 19b).

In my thinking it is to Achsah's credit that she personally asked neither for wealth nor possessions in response to Caleb's carte blanche offer, "What wouldest thou?" (Josh. 15:18). She had already, through Othniel, requested a field. Now her main desire was for water. Jesus said of the Holy Spirit and his fullness, "Out of his belly shall flow rivers of living water" (John 7:38).

The picture is obvious. The true beauty of Achsah's life, and that most obviously attractive to Othniel, was the inner radiance of her sweet spirit. It is that characteristic which still most graciously adorns the charm of God's set-apart women. And how anxious he is to fulfill the request of such a hungry and longing heart.

The sixteenth chapter describes the land chosen by lot to the sons of Joseph, who selected secondly. Ephraim's inheritance is recorded in verses 5-10, and Manasseh's, in chapter 17, verses 1-11.

Specific incidents surrounding the position of Manasseh's territory will serve as the occasion for the beginning of events in the subsequent chapter.

12
Lessons in Living

Joshua 17:1-18

The lessons of Joshua are as rich as they are manifold. God is to be obeyed at all costs. Evil must not come into the camp. The battle must be pressed to its extremities. Satan knows the Word and will use it against us. The Father is careful to point out our enemics. We are colaborers with him as we appropriate Calvary's victory. The lesson to be learned in chapter 17 deals with a far more subtle kind of enemy than we have seen to date. Now it is not the Amalekites or the Gibeonites, but the children of Israel themselves who are their own worst enemy. Already we have seen a pattern developing of stopping short of victory.

So Joshua took the whole land, according to all that the Lord said unto Moses; and Joshua gave it for an inheritance unto Israel according to their divisions by their tribes. And the land rested from war (Josh. 11:23).

Now Joshua was old and stricken in years; and the Lord said unto him, Thou art old and stricken in years, and there remaineth yet very much land to be possessed (Josh. 13:1).

Now, therefore, divide this land for an inheritance unto the nine tribes, and the half tribe of Manasseh (Josh. 13:7).

These are the inheritances, which Eleazar the priest, and Joshua the son of Nun, and the heads of the fathers of the tribes of the children of Israel, divided for an inheritance by lot in Shiloh before the Lord, at the door of the tabernacle of the congregation. So they made an end of dividing the country (Josh. 19:51).

That which began as a scattered tendency had now grown to full-blown rebellion in Joseph's children. Their inheritance was too small and they were offered a second mountain on which to expand. The problem is that it was possessed by giants and they had to fight for what is theirs. But they would fight no more. They were weary of the battle. They had had enough, and they would go no further.

Every Christian comes to this point in life. Often we grow weary, not *of* the battle, but *in* the battle. The physical, spiritual, and emotional elements of a person are interrelated, and it is extremely easy to give up the fight. Paul admonishes in Galatians 6:9 to "not be weary in well doing." One of the most subtle enemies in the Christian life is not lying or lust, but indolence, the tendency to give up the fight. It is within us all. How easy it is to "throw in the towel."

As always, God's answer to trials is an even greater trial. When the children of Joseph complained that they were a mighty people and there was not room enough for them, Joshua's answer was for them to become strong enough to possess the land by fighting the battle for an even greater mountain. God's way is never escape around a trial, but strengthening his children's spiritual muscles through the effort of even greater trials. The giants with chariots of iron can and must be conquered. Nothing is impossible with God, and no trial is without his divine approval.

James makes it clear that the trial of our faith produces

patience (Jas. 1:3-4). It is obvious from James' statement that nothing brings us to Christian maturity like the acquisition of patience. How is patience to be gained? In the midst of trial. A trial is something that has no answer. If there is a solution, we simply change the circumstances and the trial is over. But a trial is something that cannot be changed, a problem with no solution. In such a trial God's answer is always the same— Wait, have faith. Let patience have her perfect work (v. 4). The classic statement of Scripture on the subject of testing is 1 Corinthians 10:13. "There hath no temptation [trial] taken you but such as is common to man: but God is faithful, who will not suffer you to be tempted above that ye are able; but will with the temptation also make a way to escape, that ye may be able to bear it."

The expression in the King James Version, "a way to escape," is a poor translation from the Greek. God's answer is never a pathway out of the trial. The word may be better translated, "victory through the middle," for that is always the way of God. Trials are sent to make us strong, and victory is to be found by going through the trial with God. It is not his way to deliver us from Galilee's storms, but rather to come to us in their midst and give us the strength to endure. Daniel was saved *in* the lions' den, not *out* of it. The three Hebrew children were not rescued *from* the fiery furnace, but found the presence of the Son of God *in* that inferno.

The causes of Manasseh's and Ephraim's refusal to go further may be clearly seen.

1. *The Enemy Was Allowed to Live (17:12).* Whether the problem be one of discouragement, indolence, or outright sin, the result is always the same—the enemy has been allowed to live. Verse 13 states that the children of Israel "put the Canaanites to tribute." They controlled them like slaves and

made them obey and pay taxes to them. But the command was not to control, but to annihilate. The cancer of evil requires drastic surgery, and the seeds of compromise remain to produce the seed of death.

2. *Their Eyes Were on the Problem, Not the Problem Solver* (17:16-18). "We are a great people," they cried. But would to God they had added, "But greater is the Lord!" "There are chariots of iron in the land," they complained. Would to God they had added, "But God is greater still!" When Peter walked on the water, he was safe as long as he kept his eyes on Jesus. "But when he saw the wind, . . . he was afraid; and [began] to sink" (Matt. 14:30). The tendency to give up comes when we look away from the Master and look to the wind.

3. *They Were Obviously Physically and Emotionally Exhausted and Thought They Had Good Reason to Give Up the Fight.* But God strikes no bargains, grants no furloughs, gives no deals, allows no exceptions.

4. *There Was the Problem of Pride.* The basis of their argument was, "Why hast thou given [us] but one lot and one portion . . . seeing [we are] a great people, forasmuch as the Lord hath blessed [us]" (v. 14). They obviously believed that their numerical strength was in itself related to God's favor. It may be further assumed that they thought themselves to be special because they were personally related to Joshua, for he himself had come from the tribe of Ephraim (Num. 13:8).

Regardless of the magnitude of the problem, the consequences were the same and their inexcusable indolence devastating. At all costs we must never give up. We must never fail to press the battle to the very gates of hell. Our Lord places a high opinion on the importance of Christian persistence. The value of a kind of "holy hangin'-in-there" cannot be overstated. In Luke 11, Jesus illustrates this truth with the story of a person whose persistent asking at midnight was rewarded simply because he would not give up. The verb forms in his resultant statement, "Ask and it shall be given you; seek, and ye shall find; knock and it shall be opened unto you" (v. 9), are in the aorist future perfect tense—keep on knocking, keep on asking, keep on seeking, for God is a rewarder of them who diligently seek him.

When Thomas Edison's experimental laboratory was destroyed in a Christmas Eve fire, he responded, "Thank God! Twenty thousand mistakes have been burned up!" General Gobles and his men had worked more than two years to dig the Panama Canal when an earthquake pushed the millions of tons of dirt back into the hole. A newspaper reporter asked the old general what he was going to do. "Do?" the General replied. "We are going to dig it out again—what do you think we are going to do?"

For the believer there is no option. We dig out the trench and start again. We take a hitch in our belt and go forward. We pick up the struggle and fight the good fight of faith. No recesses allowed. No furlough given in our commitment to our heavenly Joshua, the Lord Jesus Christ.

13
How to Deal with a Problem

Joshua 18:1 to 19:51

The tendency to give up, expressed by the tribes, and the slackness shown by Ephraim and Manasseh had now grown to open, united opposition to the leadership of Joshua. To the man, the remaining tribes refused to go further. It was at once the final and most severe test in the life of Joshua. Much may be learned as we analyze Joshua's particular style of leadership in that crisis situation. Keep in mind that the principles by which he took charge of Israel's affairs are those by which we must allow our Lord to reign over the kingdoms of our hearts.

1. *Joshua Assumed the Leadership That Had Been Granted Him By God and Instantly and Aggressively Took Charge of the Situation.* Joshua did not wait to get on the defensive; he aggressively went on the offensive. He did not wait to respond, he acted decisively. He called the people together and demanded of them, "How long are ye slack to go to possess the land?" (18:3). It is characteristic of leadership that it is willing to run the risk of being wrong in order to express the courage

to be right. If you would avoid criticism, say nothing, do nothing, be nothing! The price of leadership is often risk and isolation; but it is to be understood that if you can't stand the heat, you should stay out of the kitchen! The Chinese proverb has said it well, "He who travels fastest, travels alone."

2. *He Recognized the Problem.* There was no question in Joshua's mind as to the precise nature of the situation. The seven remaining tribes were acting collectively and what were they doing? Precisely nothing! No need to beat around the bush. The man had the facts and the charge was clear. "How long are ye slack to go to possess the land?" We are ill-prepared to act decisively until we have taken time to carefully assimilate our information.

Joshua's plan for the people was that they, too, would come to grasp a full appreciation of all that was theirs. "Go and walk through the land, and describe it" (v. 8), was his directive. He had the facts and wanted the people to know them. There was no question in Joshua's mind as to who he was, who they were, where they were, what was to be lost in hesitation, and what was to be gained in decisive action. The time to act was now, and the courage of bold decisiveness was possible only on the basis of full information.

3. *He Made a Decision to Move the Presence of God to the Center of Canaan.* The tabernacle was moved from Gilgal at the edge of the land to Shiloh, its center. The tabernacle was the representation of the presence of God to them. There God would meet with his people at the point of innocent blood sprinkled on the mercy seat. The things of God had to be brought to the center of community life. It is always good to make a tangible, visible expression of the intent of one's heart. Baptism does that. Martin Luther's nailing his Ninety-five Theses to the door of the castle church did that. Just as one

may throw one's bottle into the river as an expression of one's intent to give up alcohol, this first visible act, as an expression of the intention of the heart, was most important.

4. *He Called the People Back to God.* When the tabernacle was moved to the heart of the land, the congregation was called before the Lord (v. 1). The call back to God must be at the center of the life of one who is earnest in his commitment to Jehovah God.

5. *He Presented the Charge in No Uncertain Terms.* "If the trumpet give an uncertain sound, who shall prepare himself to the battle?" (1 Cor. 14:8). Let there be no question in anyone's mind that Joshua said what he meant and meant what he said. The psalmist repeatedly added himself, speaking to himself as "my soul." Sometimes we have to take charge of ourselves and give ourselves a good talking to.

6. *He Has a Plan.* The people were to walk through the land as a committee of twenty-one, three from each of the seven remaining tribes. The land was to be divided into seven parts, a description made, a report returned, and a drawing held.

It is not sufficient for us merely to give ourselves a good talking to and resolve to do better. There must be a specific plan of action—what changes are going to be made, what will be left behind, and what is to be begun? If church attendance, daily prayer, witnessing, and regular Bible study are not in the plan, we will be sure that difficulties will arise.

One cannot help being impressed with the decisive nature of this take-charge attitude (v. 4—"I will, . . . they shall"; v. 5—"They shall, . . . Judah shall, . . . Joseph shall"; v. 6—"Ye shall"). Here was a man in control of himself and in control of his life. It is a kind of boldness that only the Lord can give.

In the remainder of this chapter and chapter 19, the land is surveyed, the drawing held, and the division made. The lot for Benjamin is described in chapter 18, verses 11-28; the lot for Simeon, in chapter 19, verses 1-9; the lot for Zebulun, verses 10-16; the lot for Issachar, verses 17-23; the lot for Asher, verses 24-31; the lot for Naphtali, verses 32-39.

Within chapter 19 are three seemingly incidental stories fraught with great truth. We shall look at them in reverse order to form a sequence of understanding for ourselves.

First, in verses 49-50 the children of Israel allowed Joshua the choice of any city in the land. Though he had made no demands, he received at their grateful hands his choice of all their possessions. "[Anything] which he asked" (v. 50) was their unanimous desire. The final and longest step to peace in the land of our heart comes when we offer our heavenly Joshua the right to rule where he will in the kingdom of our heart.

Second, in verse 47, there is a lovely picture of the normal Christian life. The tribe of Dan had learned well the principles of Christian victory. They went up against the enemy of Leshem and without hesitation or excuse, promptly went forward, fought against it, took it, and annihilated it. It is possible to do this only when the heavenly Joshua has been firmly settled in the land of the believer's heart.

Third, one brief, but powerful story remains from verse 9. Unlike the children of Joseph whose land was too small, the tribe of Judah found their possession too large. And, Simeon, the smallest of the tribes, was allowed to take their possession of the abundance of Judah. "Our Lord sprang out of Juda" (Heb. 7:14). The abundant, inexhaustible sufficiency of God's grace for us poor, insignificant, Simeon-like sinners may be seen clearly in this incident. No matter who you are, regardless of your weakness or the magnitude of your struggle, there is more than sufficiency in Jesus.

Whatever you need, if you enthrone Jesus as Lord, you may go from victory to victory in the daily normality of the Christian life and all that you really need to know is that he, who provides grace upon grace, is for all times "adequate!"

14
Jesus:
Our City of Refuge

Joshua 20:1-9

This record concerning the cities of refuge is a restatement of the account regarding manslaughter given in Numbers 35. The civil law laid down several qualifications regarding the relationship to crime and its punishment. For one thing, the motive must be taken into consideration. For another, the punishment must match the crime. Accidental crimes were to be treated with mercy.

> He that smiteth a man, so that he die, shall be surely put to death. And if a man lie not in wait, but God deliver him into his hand; then I will appoint thee a place whither he shall flee. But if a man come presumptuously upon his neighbour, to slay him with guile; thou shalt take him from mine altar, that he may die (Ex. 21:12-14).

In the heat of emotion following the killing of a loved one, a relative might quite naturally wreak unrestrained wrath upon the one at whose hand death had come. Under such conditions, our Lord instituted "cities of refuge" to which the slayer might flee to find safety from an avenger until the time a proper investigation and trial could be held.

These "cities of refuge" are a marvelous picture of the refuge that is to be found in "The Rock of Ages." Jesus is a "very present help in trouble" (Ps. 46:1); a "refuge from the storm" (Isa. 25:4). Much insight is to be gained into Christ our refuge by understanding the qualifications prescribed for the institution and use of these cities. Let us look at two important factors relating to them, the circumstances of their placement and use, and the meanings of their names.

Let us examine pictures of the coming of Christ into the world in his appointed ministry as sin-bearer.

1. *They Were Appointed by God Himself.* No human effort went into the preparation of the body of the Lord Jesus Christ. "That which is conceived in her," spake the angel Gabriel to Joseph of Mary, "is of the Holy Ghost" (Matt. 1:20). At the basis of all liberal theology is the tendency to deify man and humanize God. The crux of all of the world's theories of salvation may be boiled down to, "Is salvation by grace or by works?" Everything within man says, "exalt thyself." "Ye shall be as Gods" (Gen. 3:5). But it is ever the story of divine condescension that "the great Creator became my Savior." Man has no more to do with God's provision in Christ than with the attainment of his own salvation. It is, has been, and ever shall be the exclusive work of the Father to instigate and consummate the redemption of the lost human race.

2. *Each City of Refuge Provided Shelter from the Avenger.* Here the angry accuser could not reach. Here no accusations would be heard. Here the condemnation of guilt would be forever silenced. It is not man's way, for God's way never is. "God hath chosen the foolish things of the world to confound the wise" (1 Cor. 1:27). He did not clothe his Son in priestly robes but the shepherds found Jesus "wrapped in swaddling clothes, lying in a manger" (Luke 2:12). Not in fortresses built with hands, but in the Deity of a tiny babe, would God build a

mighty fortress against Satan's railing accusations. In Jesus, faith provides a shield through which the fiery darts of the wicked one may not penetrate. Before this King demons bow and Satan lies prostrate, whimpering like a scolded puppy.

3. *Each City Could Be Easily Seen*. Every city of refuge was placed high atop a hill. Our Lord intended that there be no question where the city was located and how to find it. He who is plenteous in mercy and slow to anger would provide the place of safety such that it would be readily seen by all in need of its sheltering walls. On that glorious night when the very heavens exploded with praise, there shone a light from heaven, guiding the great kings and the lowly shepherds to the precise place where the Christ child lay. As the apostle Paul said, "This thing was not done in a corner" (Acts 26:26). Born beneath a dazzling star, confirmed at the outset of his earthly ministry by the voice of God and the presence of the Spirit, followed by friend and foe, and finally crucified on a cross, our Lord from the beginning to the end of his life, made certain that all might see and know the refuge that was in God's Son.

4. *The Road Was Clearly Marked*. The signs that pointed to each of the cities were carefully maintained by the Levitical priests. In a moment of urgency a man in need of a city of refuge must not become confused. The birth of the Lord Jesus Christ as God's eternal place of refuge is, as well, clearly documented from Scripture. "For unto you is born this day in the city of David a Saviour, which is Christ the Lord" (Luke 2:11), was the clear fulfillment of the promise in Micah 5:2. John the Baptist introduced him in no uncertain terms, clearly marking the way to him as "the Lamb of God, which taketh away the sin of the world" (John 1:29).

5. *Each City Was Well Located*. The cities were evenly distributed at the centers of the population masses of the newly settled tribes. Whatever might be the point of each man's need,

111

the location of the provision for that need was not far away. Our Lord's birth in the Middle East was at the heart of civilization. The Wise Men and shepherds who came to adore him mirrored a complete cross-section of civilization. All are represented before him who would both minister and die in a public place, and who would send his disciples "into all the world, and preach the gospel to every creature" (Mark 16:15).

On the Day of Pentecost when the New Testament church was formed, Luke was careful to record that there were dwelling in Jerusalem, "devout men, out of every nation under heaven" (Acts 2:5). Every effort would be made on God's part to make provision in the refuge of his Son accessible to all. With 90 percent of the Christian work done in North America with only 10 percent of the world's population, while 10 percent minister to the other 90 percent, one must wonder if we have done as well.

6. *The Purpose of the City Was to Protect the Penitent, Not the Presumptive.* Here the analogy breaks down a bit, for our Lord is merciful and faithful to cast out none of them who "come unto me." But David prayed, "Keep back thy servant from presumptuous sins" (Ps. 20:13). The malicious, premeditated attacker would soon be found out and judged. The purpose of the refuge of Christ's cross is not to provide continuing grace in order that sin may abound; it is to make innocent the guilty who come in true contrition under the protection of his cleansing grace. Those who came to view the Christ child must kneel down to view him. The proud and unbending can never see his face.

7. *It Was Available to Jew and Gentile Alike.* It is likely that the kings of the East were Gentiles, and that the shepherds were humble Jews. His life touched all men. He died for "whosoever will." He broke down the middle wall of partition between us, making Jew and Gentile one. In Christ we are

neither Jew nor Gentile, Greek nor barbarian, male nor female. We are "one in the Spirit and one in the Lord."

8. *The Refugee Had to Remain in the Appointed Place.* Once the refugee went outside those walls, he could never return. Once he left, he was "fair game" to any who caught him and killed him. On that "night of nights" our Lord provided one place that the Savior might be found. Surely other lights shone in the heavens, and perhaps some nearly as bright. But God appointed only one star to guide all the world to one place to find his one and only "begotten Son." The swaddling clothes he wore were to be a sign, and an unusual sign at that, for swaddling clothes are grave clothes, and to find a newborn so wrapped was an interesting thing. But him in whom was eternal life had come for the exclusive purpose of death. He was born to die. Far beyond the manger, or even that wondrous night, stretched the shadow of the cross. From his birth he was marked for death.

As God would only meet his people at the point of perfect blood sprinkled on the mercy seat, so he who told Moses, "when I see the blood, I will pass over you" (Ex. 12:13), has provided salvation in "none other name under heaven given among men," there is no safety within the church or the waters of baptism or the shelter of a good life. The appointed place of refuge against the wrath of God is beneath the cleansing protection of the blood of his Son.

9. *The Safety of the Refugee Was Assured by the Life of the High Priest.* It appears that a man might stay in a city of refuge until he was willing to stand trial. However, if the trial was not heard before the death of the high priest, he could remain safely within the city for years before the high priest died. When that death occurred, he was safe to leave and live freely. The analogous relationship to our High Priest, Jesus, while mirrored here, is not an adequate one. Though he died to give

113

us our freedom, as was provided in their high priest, our High Priest, though he died, lives still and will never die. We are, therefore, cleansed by his crucifixion for our sins and eternally justified by his resurrection and intercession.

When Jesus Christ was born, he did not just begin to exist. When he died, he did not cease to live. We often see on tombstones that someone was born in a certain year and died in a certain year. But eternity cannot place a tombstone on Jesus' grave—"Born Jerusalem, 0," and "died AD 33." He is the great "I Am." He transcends both birth and death. He always was coequal with God the Father, and always will be, for he said, "He that hath seen me hath seen the Father" (John 14:9).

A final word should be written regarding the names of the cities listed here. Three cities were appointed in Canaan: Kedesh, Shechem, and Hebron. On the other side of Jordan was Bezer, Ramoth, and Golan. The names of the cities are perfect pictures of the refuge provided by our Lord Jesus, our eternal city of refuge.

1. Kedesh Implies "Holiness." The word means a sacred or holy place, a sanctuary. The righteousness of a holy God requires nothing less than absolute holiness. It is the epitome of folly for foolish man to attempt to hide himself in the unholiness of his own character or the inadequacy of man's doctrine, or even of the church and its ordinances. "Be ye holy as I am holy," saith the Lord. Man's holiness, the holiness provided by God, is an imputed one given to him on the basis of faith in his righteousness.

2. Shechem Means "Shoulder of Strength" or "Place of Strength." Jesus is our strength. He, the place of victory. When we are weak, he is strong. When we stumble, he picks us up. When we are hurt, he carries us like a shepherd. When we can bear no more and go no farther, his grace is sufficient.

3. Hebron Implies "Fellowship." It literally means union.

The greatest need of man is to have fellowship with the Father. God created man with an empty spot—a God shaped vacuum that nothing else can fill. Most of all our needs, we need him. On the cross he opened a fountain of cleansing that we might know him, whom to know is to have abundant life. He who said, "He who believeth . . . out of his belly shall flow river's living water" (John 8:38), poured out his life for us that he might pour out his life unto us. The Son of God became a Son of man that the sons of man might become sons of God.

4. Bezer Implies "A Precious Place," or "Place of Safety." It means gold or silver ore. "A mighty fortress is our God." There is no problem he cannot solve; no enemy he cannot defeat; no circumstance he cannot overcome; no need he cannot satisfy. He only asks that he be Lord of all, for he cannot do his perfect work for us until we take "hands off" of our lives and let him be Lord.

5. Ramoth Implies "Exaltation." Ramoth means a high place or height. Paul said, "Know ye not that we will judge angels" (1 Cor. 6:3). And Peter added, "If we suffer, we shall also reign with him" (2 Tim. 2:12). Here we are exalted to sonship. In the millennial reign we shall be exalted to rulership in heaven, exalted to heirship as joint heirs with Jesus Christ. All things are ours at the Father's hand and he who lavished gifts upon us, has yet in store the greatest gift of all—the gift of exaltation to eternal fellowship with the Father.

6. Golan Means "Exile" or "Immigration." Those who sought the cities of refuge were, in a sense, exiled from their original places of abode. Exiled but joyful that they had found a "blessed hiding place," free of accusation and fear of retribution. What a portrayal of the sinner in exile from the Heavenly Father. As with all of the cities of refuge, Golan paints the picture of the sinner finding his refuge, rest, and redemption in Jesus Christ, our refuge and strength.

15
Peace in the Land

Joshua 21:1 to 22:34

The last chapter restated the provision for the "cities of refuge" as required under the law and specified in Numbers. The twenty-first chapter details the specific cities for the Levites, also as prescribed under the Mosaic law. To remind Joshua that the promise of God was their unique provision (vv. 1-2), and their faith as well, God honored that promise by granting of their requests. We have only to remind God of his promises, meet the conditions, and claim the provision in faith. There we will remind ourselves of the similarities of the provision for the priests as a corollary to the church's upkeep for their gospel ministers as outlined by Paul in 1 Corinthians 9:13-14. "Do ye not know that they which minister about holy things live of the things of the temple? and they which wait at the altar are partakers with the altar? Even so hath the Lord ordained that they which preach the gospel should live of the gospel."

In an important sense, the similaries of the priests to those of the gospel minister are seen. All of their earthly needs were provided by the people they served, even to the homes in which they lived. But here the similarity ends. For one thing, the gospel minister is not called to minister to God for the people, only to minister the Word of God to the people. There is one mediator between God and man, the man—Christ Jesus. Further, they had no commission to go forth and evangelize. And perhaps most important of all, they were Levitical priests by birth, whereas the calling of a minister of God is precisely that, a divine calling based upon no human succession.

(Read Joshua 22:1-34.)

In the first six verses of chapter 22, Joshua released the two and one-half tribes to return to their chosen inheritance on the other side of Jordan. They had "kept the charge" (v. 3) to assist their brethren in conquering the land, and now could go back to their inheritance.

> For our light affliction, which is but for a moment, worketh for us a far more exceeding and eternal weight of glory; While we look not at the things which are seen, but at the things which are not seen: for the things which are seen are temporal; but the things which are not seen are eternal. For we know that if our earthly house of this tabernacle were dissolved, we have a building of God, an house not made with hands, eternal in the heavens (2 Cor. 4:17-18 to 5:1).

The command to recross Jordan and to possess their possessions was given to the two and one-half tribes in the seventh year. As the number seven represents completion, the seventh year speaks of the finality of their victory as they are safely settled in.

In the fifth and sixth verses, Joshua sent them away with a most beautiful charge. "As Moses . . . charged you, to love the Lord your God, and walk in all his ways; and to keep his commandments, and to cleave unto him; and to serve him with all your heart and with all your soul" (v. 5). If no other verse existed in the Bible, this one would more than adequately express the secret of a happy and successful life.

As they left, they were rewarded with every provision needed to begin life in their new inheritance (v. 8). There is an obvious abundance from him who "shall supply all your need according to his riches in glory by Christ Jesus" (Phil. 4:19).

The remainder of the chapter speaks of the earnest commitment of the nine and one-half tribes to the integrity of the law. Upon crossing the river, the two and one-half tribes built a monument near the site the original "Monument of Stones" was placed, marking the initial crossing of the Jordan. Upon learning of the erection of such an altar, the nine and one-half tribes assumed the possibility of defection. Were the two and one-half tribes already turning from the clear command of Jehovah to build no other altars for sacrifice? Such could not be allowed. They were still blood brothers and what a few did would affect them all. The purity of the faith had to be maintained, the integrity of the law upheld, and continual commitment to God's laws maintained at all costs.

Immediately a council was held, and an investigatory party was sent to call the two and one-half tribes to account. The gratifying result of the confrontation set at ease the minds of the investigators. No such idolatry was intended. The reasoning of the two and one-half tribes was that one day their children would ask who were those peoples across Jordan in the land of Canaan. The altar was intended only as an eternal monument to the descendants of the two and one-half tribes that though they were separated by a river; the entire twelve tribes formed a unit of unilateral commitment to Jehovah God. "God forbid that we should rebel against the Lord, . . . and build an altar for burnt offerings" (v. 29). The sole purpose for the building was a monument to the unity of the tribes under the one true God. The investigators returned to share the good news at Shiloh and the land was at peace.

On the one hand, we commend the two and one-half tribes for their zeal and desire to perpetuate the faith to successive generations. On the other, we must equally praise the immediate response of the nine and one-half tribes to deal with any potential defection. The Christian education of our children is the best means by which the purity of the gospel may be maintained. The religious education of our children is primary to the Christian faith. The church must be zealous in discipling her own.

16
We Will Serve the Lord!

Joshua 23:1 to 24:33

The closing two chapters of Joshua includes his farewell address and challenge to the tribes. His departing messages in the two chapters are given to two different groups and recount their historical victories from two perspectives. Chapter 23 was delivered only to the leaders of the tribes. The place was Shiloh, and the subject was the recounting of "all the Lord your God hath done" since they came into the land of Canaan (v. 3).

The lecture in chapter 24 was delivered at Shechem to all the children of Israel and was a challenge to go forward in light of all that had been done since the very beginning when "I took your father Abraham from the other side of the flood . . . and gave him Isaac" (v. 3).

Joshua was old and well-stricken in years. He was one hundred and ten years of age (24:29). Caleb claimed to be as young at eighty-five as at forty. If Caleb were a young eighty-five, Joshua was an old one hundred ten. The years had been long and had taken a severe toll on the leader. The forty years in the wilderness, the intensity of the campaigns, the responsibilities of leadership, and the passing of years had left their mark. Many got sidetracked in their later years—Moses, Samson, and Solomon. It is noteworthy that Joshua was faithful unto death.

Soon Joshua would be gone and they would have to stand on their own. People come and go, but the work of the Lord will endure. It was this fact that they had to understand. It was not Joshua who had won the battles—that honor goes to Jehovah and he is Jehovah the Lord, your God. No second-hand faith would sustain them through the time to come. He who was Joshua's God must be their God. The undershepherd faithfully points the flock to the heavenly Shepherd. Twice in verse 3 it is "the Lord your God." Twice more in verse 5 the emphasis is repeated, "The Lord your God, he shall expel them, . . . as the Lord your God hath promised unto you." "Cleave unto the Lord your God" (v. 8). And again in verses 10-11, second-hand faith will not do. He, by whose hand Jehovah had delivered Israel, would soon be gone. But Jehovah changes not, and it was he who must be the object of their faith.

In verses 6-16 the people were warned against the blight of apostasy. They had recently dealt with the potential of its dastardly roots and must never be overtaken by it unawares.

The tendency among the sons of Joseph to go no further in chapter 17 had spread to all the tribes in chapter 18. The warning against apostasy was a warning against going back. That which had happened before must never happen again (v. 12). The possibility of amalgamation with the heathen nations whom they had conquered weighed heavily upon Joshua's mind. He refers to: "these nations," verses 3-4, 7, 12-13; "them," verse 5; "great nations," verse 9.

Too many lessons had been learned, too much blood spilled, too much heartache experienced, too much land conquered, too much progress made to turn back now. It is terrible to turn back. "Ever onward," is the cry of the Christian army! "I'm pressing on the upward way, New heights I'm gaining ev'ry day," should ever be the earnest prayer of the Christian.

The results of defecting are clearly stated by Joshua in a fourfold outline:

1. **Defeat.** "Know for a certainty that the Lord your God will no more drive out any of these nations from before you" (v. 13a). Let there be no question, the victory Israel had enjoyed had been secured by obedience to Jehovah. Faithfulness equals victory, and apostasy means defeat.

2. **Discomfort.** "They shall be snares and traps to you and scourges in your sides, and thorns in your eyes" (v. 13b). Misery and sorrow await the faithless. A compromising Christian will not be a happy one.

3. **Disintegration.** The Lord shall "[destroy] you from off this good land" (v. 15).

4. **Disgrace.** "The anger of the Lord shall be kindled against you" (v. 16). The very Lord who fought for them will now fight against them. Let it be well remembered that our Lord will arrange the affairs of entire nations and of the very elements of the universe themselves to support the person who is moving with God. But one who sets oneself against Jehovah, sets oneself against the very order of things and ensures one's own disgrace and defeat.

Within the warning there is included a threefold safeguard for Israel. The first safeguard is obedience. The children of Israel are to "keep and do all that is written in the book of the law" (23:6). From Genesis to Revelation, the key word to victory, joy, and success is *obedience*!

The second key is separation. Not only was there to be no collusion with the evil one, they were not to so much as "make mention of the name of their gods" (v. 7). No quarter must be given, no alliance made, not so much as the tip of a hat allowed toward the idolatrous paganism of the secular world. At all costs it is still, "Come out from among them, and be ye separate, saith the Lord, and touch not the unclean thing; and I will receive you" (2 Cor. 6:17).

The third safeguard is to "love the Lord your God" (v. 11). To obey God is to love him. To "love the Lord" is an expression that is unique to Moses and Joshua. These two Old Testament saints lived so close to Jehovah that the first dawning rays of the truth of an understanding of what it meant to truly know God and love him first began to shine in their hearts. Jesus said that the essence of all the law and the prophets was to "love the Lord thy God with all thy heart and with all thy soul, and with all thy mind. Thou shalt love thy neighbor as thyself" (Matt. 22:37,39). To obey God is to separate yourself from the service of others. To obey God is to love him. We cannot be neutral. God and mammon may not at once be served. "What concord hath Christ with Belial?" (2 Cor. 6:15).

His appeal was to the whole man. The first challenge was to the mind. It was a commitment to Israel to make up their minds to act. The Israelites had good sense. They had obviously seen what courageous and brave action would do. It follows that courageous men should express a willingness to do what makes men brave, and that is to act! The challenge was to have the courage to act decisively in instantaneous obedience.

His second appeal was to the will. A commitment must be made. God must be chosen. Therefore, "cleave unto the Lord your God" (v. 8). The alternative was to "cleave unto the remnant of these nations [and die]" (v. 12).

The final appeal was to Israel's emotion. Let God be the object of their affections. "Take heed . . . that ye love the Lord your God" (v. 11). No more stirring message was ever given. There is rhetoric, history, challenge, reminder, application, instruction, and appeal to mind, emotion, and will. All of this leads quite naturally to the final challenge of chapter 24. "Choose you this day whom ye will serve" (24:15).

In chapter 24 the gathering of all the people to Shechem occurs (v. 1). It is noteworthy that Shechem was the valley between Mount Ebal and Mount Gerizim where Joshua had addressed them before, and where they had so dramatically repeated both the cursings and blessings of the law. There an altar to the Lord had been built with all the law recorded thereon (ch. 8). Here the great man of God presumed to speak for Jehovah. "Thus saith the Lord" (v. 2), the reiteration of their history from Abraham is given in the first person. Joshua spoke of God: "I took" (v. 3); "I gave" (v. 4); "I sent" (v. 5); "I brought" (v. 6). What an encouragement it was to the people to review all that God had done for them. An equal synopsis of victory is recounted for the New Testament believer in Hebrews 11.

The key word to this section is the word *therefore* in verse 14. Because what Joshua has said was true, it was also true that God had the right to demand a response. He had recounted what he had done and now demanded to know what they would do. The purpose of all religious discourse is to move us from inspiration to motivation—from instruction to decision. Paul's writings abound with this truth. Always in the first person he teaches doctrine, then exhorts to the corresponding duty in the latter part. No teaching, no instruction is complete without exhortation and invitation. Jesus' seven letters to the churches in Revelation make clear the principle.

In response to his demand for a verdict, the people responded in the affirmative, "God forbid that we should forsake the Lord, to serve other gods" (v. 16). Joshua's response to their response was very significant. He used a kind of holy provoking, saying to them, "Ye cannot serve the Lord" (v. 19). Joshua was saying, "You say that you are doing it, but you will never do it. I know you and God knows you, and you will never do what you say." His unique technique was most successful. "And the people said unto Joshua, Nay; but we will serve the Lord" (v. 21)!

Following this second affirmation, Joshua immediately instructed the people to memorialize their commitment with the erection of a great statue of stone (vv. 25-26). We have repeatedly seen the importance of such tangible expressions of eternal commitment. Joshua intended that at the center of the life of Israel would stand a perpetual monument to their unalterable commitment to Jehovah. Verses 29 through 33 are a simple statement of the death and burial of Joshua, of Eleazar, the high priest; and of the burial of the bones of Joseph brought out of Egypt.

The name Joshua means "Jehovah is salvation." Joseph means "[Jehovah] may he add." Eleazar means "God hath helped." Together, the close of the book of Joshua is a benediction of praise to the faithfulness of God, and may be clearly seen in a combination of these three names: "Jehovah, who has saved us out of Egypt and out of the wilderness, has added to us the land of his faithful promise and shall ever be our help."